THE MIRACLE OF COPENHAGEN

ARSENAL'S UNBELIEVABLE EUROPEAN CUP WINNERS' CUP RUN AND TRIUMPH

Layth Yousif

*Dedicated to the memory of Robert 'Benjy' Ansell, 1972 –2005.
True friend to all and true Gooner. I hope this book answers
your question about The Miracle of Copenhagen.
Rest in peace, mate.*

Passages of this book have appeared in *The London Evening Standard,
The Islington Gazette, The Gooner* fanzine and *Sabotage Times*.

First published 2016

Amberley Publishing
The Hill, Stroud
Gloucestershire, GL5 4EP

www.amberley-books.com

British Library Cataloguing in Publication Data.
A catalogue record for this book is available from the British Library.

ISBN 978 1 4456 4949 8 (print)
ISBN 978 1 4456 4950 4 (ebook)

Typesetting and Origination by Amberley Publishing.
Printed in the UK.

Contents

About the Author

Layth Yousif is a journalist and author. He has been watching Arsenal since the early '80s and has had a season ticket for more than three decades. He freelances for the online sports desk of the *London Evening Standard*, and has written for *When Saturday Comes*, *Four Four Two*, *World Soccer*, and many other sporting publications. He also writes an Arsenal column for the *Islington Gazette* and is a regular contributor to *The Gooner* Fanzine. *The Miracle of Copenhagen* is his second book with Amberley, following *Arsène Wenger: 50 Defining Fixtures*. Born and bred Londoner Layth now resides in the Hertfordshire market town of Hitchin with his partner, and their three Junior Gunners. Follow him on Twitter and Instagram: @laythy29

Foreword

It's so difficult, isn't it? To see what's going on when you're in the absolute middle of something? It's only with hindsight we can see things for what they are.

S. J. Watson, *Before I Go To Sleep*

European football in 1994 was a nirvana Arsenal fans were simply not used to tasting. Looking back from where we are more than two decades later, in a situation where qualifying for the Champions League annually is normal, some history and context is necessary to put the campaign into perspective. By today's standards the Winners' Cup would not appear to carry an awful lot of weight. At a time when the Europa League is underestimated, and even unwelcome, for some English clubs. A competition that was regarded as one rung lower in the trophy hierarchy, which lost its status to the point where it became defunct, might struggle to convince people who have only read about it in history books how much it mattered. But it has to be judged in its moment. Given Arsenal's experience of European football at that time, its significance in 1994 was huge. It was not long after the period of banishment in the aftermath of the Heysel disaster which kept English clubs out of European competition. To have a foreign odyssey of any kind was very meaningful.

Arsenal missed out on a season in the European Cup in 1989 because of the ban. Two years later in 1991 when the club returned to continental competition the experience was relatively short lived as they only played two rounds, home and away, seeing off Austria Vienna before absorbing a tough lesson from Benfica. Four matches, that's it. A simple calculation speaks volumes about how any European outing was to be cherished. In an entire decade leading up to that 1993/94 run Arsenal participated in just those four matches which took place over a handful of weeks. Other than that, the club was in the European wilderness.

To be back on that stage was very exciting in 1994. Many fans were desperate to go on trips. It offered a thrill, a sense of adventure, and a tension that came with the knowledge that travelling abroad for English fans had an unavoidable edge the legacy of hooliganism. There was no over familiarity with foreign opponents then. Finding out details about the team you were up against could be a challenge in the pre-internet, pre-global audience days. With European football now on every week with every game accessible at the press of a button, you can live almost anywhere and have knowledge of different teams and different players – but that wasn't the case in the early 1990s. Information was passed by word of mouth. Travelling fans became representatives of their clubs. You no longer need to walk into a bar in some far flung place to tell anyone who might be interested about the Arsenal team because the chances are they know plenty through the modern exposure of football.

In 1993/94 George Graham and his players, and the band of supporters who followed them from their away games onto the final against Parma, carried their flag on their backs and the wind behind them.

Victory, for all those, in the European Cup Winners' Cup was momentous.

Amy Lawrence
May 2015

Prologue

Odense is one of Denmark's oldest cities. Vikings built numerous fortifications along its river banks to defend against invaders from the coast. The name Odense derives from *Odins Vé* meaning 'Odin's sanctuary' as the place was renowned as a sanctuary for worshippers of the Nordic god, Odin. The city celebrated its thousandth anniversary in 1988 commemorating the first mention of the town's name in a letter dated 18 March 988 from the German Emperor Otto III. Situated 104 miles to the south-west of the nation's capital, Copenhagen is now the third largest city in this remarkable country. Odense is also the region's most important industrial and commercial centre and businesses include the famed Albani Brewery. Faaxe beer is brewed in the east of the country with the name Fakse being Old Norse meaning 'horse mane'. And today, in the old precinct of Odense, nestled in a quaint side street known as Munkemøllestræde lies a traditional cottage house. The picturesque, yellow-walled, half-timbered house with red pan tiles on its slanted roof was once home to the city's most famous son. This humble house situated in what was a poor part of the city was where the infant was born on Tuesday 2 April 1805. His father was a cobbler. His mother, Anne Marie Andersdatter, never received an education and worked as a washerwoman following the child's death in 1816. She was also very superstitious. The lad did not gain much of an education either, but his fascination with fables and miracles inspired him to compose his own stories and arrange puppet shows on a small theatre his late father had helped build for him. The name of the youngster who would be loved and admired the world over? Hans Christian Andersen. Was there ever a more fitting place to start a run that would lead Arsenal to European glory than Odense – the home city of a writer who would grip his fans with fairy-tales that came true?

And so began on 15 September 1993 one of the biggest fairy tales ever associated with Arsenal Football Club in its long and illustrious history – a tale of triumph over adversity, of teamwork and loyalty over flair and skill, of courage and bravery beating arrogance and pride, of a band of brothers who, despite being written off as Ugly Ducklings overturned improbable odds through hard work and solidarity in achieving something no-one could have envisaged that wet September night in the birthplace of the world's greatest conjurer of fairy tales – a tale which is still spoken about now in hushed reverence by the majority of Arsenal fans across the planet: The Miracle Of Copenhagen.

As a fitting tribute each of the following chapter titles are taken from an original fairy tale written by Andersen.

1

Odense vs Arsenal:
The Galoshes of Fortune

European Cup Winners' Cup first round, first-leg. 15 September 1993. Odense 1 Arsenal 2.

> I cannot recommend this beer enough. It is refreshing, savoury and strong. Try it!
>
> Hans Christian Andersen in a letter to a friend.

> I think we, as a team under George Graham and Stewart Houston, did enjoy playing in Europe because it was a different challenge.
>
> Alan Smith in conversation with the author.

> The Cup Winners Cup was quite an attractive trophy to compete in, quite a prestigious trophy to compete for. It was a big step in the unknown for everybody. We were looking forward to the challenge. It was a new campaign for us, a new challenge and it was one we relished taking on. There was a new freshness about competing in Europe for the club.
>
> Arsenal assistant manager Stewart Houston in conversation with the author.

> My memories from the Odense game in Denmark are that it was a fantastic day with a lot of happy supporters from both clubs. Danish supporters were very proud and happy to see a big club like Arsenal playing in Denmark so the atmosphere between the fans was outstanding. We were singing together at the local pubs before and after the game. People took a lot of pictures together – all happy days!
>
> Flemming Christiansen, Danish Arsenal fan who attended the match.

The man walks in with a brisk stride, eyes alert and intelligent. His clothes are various shades of dark hues. They are modest and understated, much like the man himself, but they are expensive even if they are worn in a casual manner suggesting a man at ease with himself. Like so many successful men in so many fields his handshake is firm and his pupils fix you with a steely, non-committal stare. Yet his manner is not icy, or offhand, but one which indicates a willingness to engage, perhaps even a suggestion of empathy – but only if you earn it. There is no small talk. My friend Dan McCarthy (who I will be collaborating with on my next book, *What The Arsenal Means To Me*) genially offers to order a round of coffees for the three of us and heads off. I am left answering direct and probing questions which strike right at the heart of why the man is here. I have seconds to impress. Or at the very least not to muck up.

'Tell me about yourself,' the tall man asks. I rose instinctively when he walked in and have yet to sit down again and I am far too respectful (or is it fearful) to presume to ask him to take a seat to start our interview. I mumble a few generalities. His eyes, grey blue, with flashes of ashen gunmetal dance around following your gaze. Or trying to catch mine. I attempt to look him in the eye but my aim is slightly off centre.

Is it modesty which forbids my psyche from looking directly into the eyes of a true footballing legend? Is it the fact I still can't believe I am here or is it the fact that twenty-one years ago, two short decades with a myriad of personal triumphs, disasters and banalities under my belt, the man I am standing talking to provided me with one of the highlights of my life. Just for a moment think about what your life would be like if you didn't like sport.

Not just the glorious game of football but of any sport. Any game you care passionately about. If you have never expected the absolute high of a moment granted to you by a hero who wears your team's colours, who represents your team – who is your team. A person who transcends the drudgery of your own life by elevating the entity you love into a winning team. It doesn't even have to be a victory. It could be a moment of balletic, breath-taking, skill, a millisecond of joyous improvised excitement which will live with you forever. A moment of illusion as they say in Spain.

Imagine if you never lived your life without the hope, the belief, you a truly wondrous moment would make its mark on your life forever. How poor would your existence be if you did not have that? As a sports fan, as a football fan and as an Arsenal fan I am lucky enough to have sampled that elation, that delight, that true bloody rapture. Therefore when the man looked at me with ever increasing dubiousness at my failure to lock onto his eyes when speaking my opening gambit I did so only because my mind's eye was still picturing the exact moment when he scored one of the goals of my life. Not his life I grant you, although he had far more claim to it, but my life. My life as an Arsenal fan. The man was Alan Smith. The goal was the winner against Parma to win the 1993/94 European Cup Winners Cup.

Dan comes back with three coffees just as I can feel myself accelerating into a confused monologue. We all sit down and I take out the tools of my trade. A notepad for my painfully accrued shorthand and a dictaphone for back up. Alan Smith looks at them with a knowing eye, as he too is a journalist, and his eyes soften a touch with an understanding that I am serious about my job and my interview with him.

What do I call him I think to myself, Alan? Too formal. Mr Smith? Too oleaginous and ingratiating. Smudge? Too familiar. I settle for a far too chummy segue into my first question without even having the politeness to call him anything. Instead, I opt for a fall back of telling him he was – is – an Arsenal legend and ask him for his memories of that cup run, of playing in the European Cup Winners Cup that immortal season starting with Odense away. He thinks hard, underlining his reputation as someone who cares about the game passionately, who is articulate and who puts a lot of thought into whatever comes out of his mouth. The Arsenal legend replies to me by answering,

> It was different. It was harder. I was playing in a system where I was normally up front on my own so there were certain challenges with that. I think we as a team under George Graham did enjoy playing in Europe because it was a different challenge. We used to watch videos of teams we would be playing. It wasn't like playing teams you know in the same league, when you know the opposition, you know who's going to mark you. We were well prepared for the opposition. We did enjoy it. Playing on foreign grounds. We'd had that period where English clubs were banned from Europe from 1985 to 1991 so it was a new adventure for us. And playing Odense away in Denmark was a brand new adventure for us.

And it brings September 1993 rushing back in an instant. Number one in the middle of September 1993 was 'Boom! Shake the Room' by DJ Jazzy Jeff and The Fresh Prince. Sky multi-channels launches in the UK and BBC One unveil, to great expense, a new soap called Eldorado, described by one reviewer as, 'A byword for any unsuccessful, poorly received or over-hyped television show destined for failure.' It lasted exactly twelve months before it was scrapped to much derision.

Earlier, when politician Roy Hattersley fails to appear for an edition of *Have I Got News for You* (the third time he cancelled at the last minute) he is replaced with a tub of lard. Credited as The Rt Hon Tub of Lard MP because it is 'imbued with much the same qualities and liable to give a similar performance'. And on 15 September, Arsenal embarked on only their fifth competitive European football match in fourteen years. Odense away, in the first round, first-leg of the European Cup Winners' Cup trophy.

The man is stern but engaging, polite but passionate, knowledgeable and studious. His accent sounds the same as it did twenty-one years ago and his love of Arsenal remains as strong as ever. Stewart Mackie Houston, born 20 August 1949 in Dunoon, Scotland is a former football player and coach. The tough Scot was assistant manager to George Graham at Arsenal from 1990, and was twice the club's caretaker-manager, initially for three months in 1995 after the managerial incumbent George Graham's sacking in February 1995. Houston then guided the team to the final of the European Cup Winners' Cup, but the Gunners lost to a last-minute goal from Nayim.

Those are the bald facts. The details are what matter. And for that glorious run in 1993/94 he was the influential and trusted number two to Graham as the pair plotted their way through the minefield of continental opposition, eventually emerging with huge credit in even outfoxing teams from the tactically superior Italian league of Series A.

I thank him for his time and begin by stating breathlessly, I was at both games for the 1993 FA Cup Final and the celebrations after Andy Linighan's late winner were brilliant as a fan so I can only imagine what they were like for the players and management team, but at what point did it sink in and you thought we're now in the Cup Winners Cup? Stewart thinks deeply, a trait which is always impressive in football men. He draws breath then says in that familiar accent of his as the memories comes flooding back,

The FA Cup was the avenue to get through into this competition as you well know Layth – of course it's all changed now – but you've got to remember the Cup Winners Cup was quite an attractive trophy to compete in, quite a prestigious trophy to compete for. And by winning the FA Cup in such a dramatic fashion took us a step into the unknown if you like. It was a big step for everybody.

We were looking forward to the challenge. It was a new campaign for us, a new challenge and it was one we relished taking on. There was a new freshness about competing in Europe for the club. Of course we were in the European Cup in 1991 but we didn't go as far as would have liked in that tournament as we had a really good team. So 1993/94 was a chance for us to do something in Europe.

It was a huge learning curve for us all, a new era, if you like for everybody, for the club, the staff and the whole club in general. We weren't the favourites in any way shape or form, we were the ones propping up the fixtures if you like. We did approach it with a very professional attitude, and it really was a case of let's just face the obstacle immediately in front of us and see where it takes us. You can't look any further than the obstacle that's in front of you and that attitude served us well.

We certainly approached Odense in a serious manner. In those days Scandinavian teams were actually very decent sides. They were very well respected so when the draw was made there was never any sense of taking the tie lightly or thinking we were through or anything disrespectful like that. We took them seriously and treated them with respect.

Of course a Scandinavian club football hasn't been at the top of European competition over the last ten, fifteen years, but in those days they were good solid sides. We had watched Odense a few times and treated them with the respect they deserved as befits any team in the same European competition as you. That was our approach in those days.

I remember the tie but not the specifics. There was nothing that particularly stood out. I'll tell you what I remember was that George always wanted to get the team on the pitch. By that I mean he always wanted the team to train on the pitch we were going to play on in Europe. So we made sure we flew the day before the game so we could train on Odense's pitch the evening before the match. It was important for us to get a feel of the pitch as it were. Even if was light training, or simple stretching before and afterwards. It also helped in making us aware of the environment and the stadium and sample the surroundings so that there were no nasty surprises when the match started.

Ok, there would have been no-one at the stadium in Odense the night before but we, George and I, felt simply by training on the pitch the night before it gave you an appetite for the actual match. To do well in the actual match by giving you a taste of your surroundings, and getting you to focus on the game.

We would have known the final would have been played in Copenhagen because UEFA normally announced where the final was going to be a long time in advance but I don't recall there being any irony in the fact we were starting our campaign in Denmark, just outside Copenhagen and planned to finish it at the Parken Stadium in Copenhagen.

We just saw Odense as a tough stepping stone we had to overcome if we wanted to progress in the competition. I have to say at that time continental teams were recognised as having that extra bit of technical ability compared to our teams in England and that's no disrespect to our teams as we had a lot of other attributes that continental teams would have feared such as our tremendous will to win and fighting spirit, our high intensity game, and our physicality, but there was a sense of feeling that continental teams just had a bit more technical ability. Playing in Europe against teams like Odense, and as we progressed, Liège, Torino, Paris and Parma, gave us new ideas, new playing styles. And if you look at some of the teams, they had their wing-backs and three centre-backs which are quite standard now, but back then it was all new to us, all a bit different because we never came across that too much in the Premier League at the time. There were certainly plusses and minuses we had to address in terms of combating continental teams tactics, starting with Odense.

I was impressed by Stewart Houston's knowledge, and tactical nous. No wonder the team was never less than prepared to meet any opponent, whether it be familiar foes from the Premier League or unheralded opposition from unfamiliar European leagues it was reassuring to hear from a man so integral to that immortal run that Arsenal were not going to be surprised on the pitch by anyone.

For the travelling supporters however, everything was new. Former *Sky News* journalist, now a senior media and communications consultant Jem Maidment, a regular contributor to the Arsenal match day programme and huge Gooner, recalls the trip to Hans Christian Andersen's birthplace,

We had to take an official travel club coach to Denmark from Highbury, it was the cheapest option by a mile. It was a hellish journey. We got to Odense eight hours before kick-off and were not allowed to go into town for a beer, and more importantly, a wash. Not that it mattered, because it rained and rained and rained. The stadium was basic beyond belief.

I think they had even built a new stand for the occasion but I'm not sure. I do remember when Paul Merson scored the winner of what was a truly awful game, a dozen or so Arsenal fans climbed the fence in our little corner to celebrate and the whole thing came down. Talk about shoddy workmanship.

In this day and age of the Champions League and shiny modern stadiums, many fans simply would not comprehend those kind of stadiums even existed. But they did, believe me.

The editor of the much loved and much respected Arsenal fanzine *The Gooner*, Kevin Whitcher explained,

It was the first foray into Europe since the European Cup elimination at the hands of Benfica in 1991. However, in spite of only being two years on, it was a very different Arsenal, in terms of tactics, rather than personnel, which entered the European Cup Winners Cup.

The first game out of the nine that would be played in the campaign was the only one I did not attend, although listening to updates on the radio, it sounded like Arsenal made hard work of the trip to Odense, in Denmark, not too far from where they would conclude the competition a few months later. It was just as well a 2-1 victory was recorded as the game back at Highbury finished 1-1. It was an inauspicious start.

Publisher and founding editor of *The Gooner* Mike Francis added,

The first issue of *The Gooner* from the 1993/94 season featured a caricature of George Graham pulling the FA and League Cups out of his magic hat and promising to deliver the Cup Winners Cup for his next trick. It was published more in hope than expectation but it turned out to be a wonderful prophecy which would be realised in wonderful, wonderful Copenhagen.

I hadn't ventured into Europe with Arsenal before that first Cup Winners Cup run. I had been too young when we had been in Europe before the ban on English clubs in the mid-1980s and during our all too short European Cup adventure two years previously I'd passed up opportunities to go to Vienna and Benfica preferring to keep my powder dry and my money in my bank account until the group phase which awaited us after we'd overcome Benfica.

As we all know, that didn't quite turn out as planned thanks to a player called Isaías who has never quite disappeared from my nightmares. This time I was determined to enjoy a trip or two, but a young family and financial commitments meant it was not until the semi-final that I got the green light from my other half to get my passport out for the trip across the channel to watch us take on PSG. Of course before we got that far we'd had to overcome three opponents in the previous rounds. As you'd expect, *The Gooner* had ensured the trips Odense, Liège and Turin were adequately covered.

We discovered that Odense was the birthplace of Hans Christian Anderson although it transpired he left the town as soon as he got the chance and judging by Eugene Harper's trip report, we can understand why. It wasn't the liveliest of destinations and the fact it rained incessantly for the duration of Eugene's stay certainly didn't help.

Hard-core Danish Gooner Flemming Christensen was also at the Odense game. The personable Dane with a huge passion for Arsenal told me good naturedly,

I became an Arsenal Supporter when I was eleven years old as my dad took me to a game at Highbury and I have followed them ever since. I am a member of Arsenal Denmark and we are at the moment approaching 2,400 members in Denmark.

My memories from the Odense game in Denmark are that it was a fantastic day with a lot of happy supporters from both clubs. Danish supporters were very proud and happy to see a big club like Arsenal playing in Denmark so the atmosphere between the fans was outstanding. We were singing together at the local pubs before and after the game. People took a lot of pictures together. All happy days!

Guardian and *Observer* journalist Amy Lawrence, author of the best-selling book *Invincible*, who has been watching Arsenal since the 1970s told me,

I went to Odense away. I remember it poured with rain. It was a tiny little place, it really was. It was a bit like being dropped into a quite quaint little town. Scandinavia is a region where there are traditionally lots of Arsenal supporters. Where the club was and is well regarded.

George Graham would invariably take a team to Scandinavia in pre-season in those days so there was a connection there. And there was a load of Scandinavian Arsenal supporters in the ground in the away section. So there was that quite funny feeling of singing Arsenal songs – and then lots of people in very strong Scandinavian accents singing it heartily! It was great fun.

I mention talking to Fleming to Amy and that he pretty much said the same thing. Amy smiles and replied,

It was really great fun. The whole day was played out to a friendly atmosphere between the two sets of fans. I remember talking to a lot of Danish Arsenal fans and Scandinavian Arsenal fans and having a drink with them in the bars before the match. One of my friends who was there with me, a Swedish Arsenal fan who we'd met on a pre-season tour to the country a couple of years previously, met us and we all had a great time.

Ian Selley who made a start in that game was a young lad who came through the ranks and people wanted him to do well. He seemed to have a nice touch but I remember him being quite slender.

However, Arsenal shareholder and season ticket holder Darren Epstein recalled his trip to Odense via the Arsenal Travel Club,

What was weird was that we had already been through a limited European campaign, in 1991/92 when we had been to Vienna and Lisbon, but for some reason, people felt that we had a better chance in 1993/94.

Those days you weren't allowed to buy tickets separately and travel yourself, you had to buy a package from Arsenal, or make your own way there without tickets. Most people went with the club because English fans were still generally a target for troublemakers so it was somewhat easier and safer to go with them.

I hadn't travelled with the Arsenal Travel Club for years. I always find them a nightmare, but I had to for this game. We arrived and were herded to the buses, knowing that the ground was twelve miles away.

We had three hours and we thought it would be great to get a couple of hours outside the ground. Unfortunately we left the airport at a snail's pace. There were about five or six coaches from memory, and we continued at literally walking pace in convoy. Then it dawned that they were going as slow as possible as they didn't want English fans to spend too much time outside the ground. It took us like ninety minutes to get to the ground and then we were shepherded inside, couldn't mingle outside or buy anything, just treated really poorly.

That was generally the case in those days. It wasn't until fans started to see that you could buy tickets outside the ground and that there was no real need to go with the club that the away European games became fun. Odense away was literally the last time I ever went with the Arsenal Travel Club.

With a cloying pitch against a young enthusiastic team with home support the tie could have been far trickier than it turned out to be.

For Arsenal, facing their first European test since the juddering 3-1 home defeat in the European Cup to Benfica at Highbury in November 1991 it was interesting to hear what a bullish George Graham had to say at the time about that seminal defeat ahead of the match in Denmark. 'To say Benfica outplayed us is nonsense,' he roared, 'We had most of the chances. If we had put three quarters of them away we would have won easily.'

Coming up is the crucial sentence for it contained the ethos and strategy of that season's campaign,

If we learned anything, it was to be patient, especially at home. But you still have to be positive,' adding, 'the continentals withdraw, even on their home ground. If we get the ball at the back, they will just drop off, which we're not used to.

Another thing Arsenal weren't used to was conceding an early penalty. Helveg played a through ball towards Thorup but 1993 FA Cup Final goal scoring hero, centre half Andy Linighan appeared to play the ball in his challenge. Unfortunately for Arsenal, the Turkish referee, a good 20 yards behind play, decided it was a penalty.

Thankfully, Thorup was wasteful as he fired his spot kick against the outside of David Seaman's right hand post. However, in the eighteenth minute a shot from Neilsen which appeared to be going wide took a diversion off Martin Keown and into the net to make it 1-0 to the Danes. Yet the Arsenal of that vintage were renowned for their fighting spirit and never-say-die attitude. From Jensen's free kick, Nigel 'Nutty' Winterburn struck a fierce volley from outside the box and Ian Wright followed up on the rebound after keeper Hogh parried to make it 1-1 in the 36th minute.

Merson was then to receive a superb curled pass from Kevin Campbell in the sixty-ninth minute and eased past two despairing Odense defenders before striking home the winner. In a sodden stadium on a hiding to nothing Arsenal showed their resilience. It wasn't the last time they would in this run, their brand new adventure, Alan Smith told me face-to-face, had just begun.

Fans Fight as Cardiff Clash.

About 100 Cardiff fans were detained in an army barracks after clashing with Standard Liège supporters and police before last night's European Cup Winners' Cup tie in Belgium. The Welsh side lost 5–2 after leading 2–1.

The violence was the first involving British fans in Belgium since the Heysel Stadium disaster in 1985. Last night's trouble erupted outside a bar, which had also been the scene of trouble on Tuesday night.

Police broke up the fighting which involved about 200 Cardiff fans, many of them drunk. Those not arrested were escorted to the stadium where they saw a remarkable match.

Guardian, 16 September, 1993.

2

Arsenal vs Odense:
Several Things

European Cup Winners' Cup, first round, second-leg. 29 September 1993.
Arsenal 1 Odense 1. (Arsenal win 3-2 on aggregate.)

> You are a dreamer, and that is your misfortune.
>
> Hans Christian Andersen, *There is a Difference.*

> George was fantastic. George was great. He was obviously a little bit different, he was more of a person who might have a go at you if you didn't play as well as you could. George had his own style of management whereas Arsene Wenger would look at the video and pull us aside on the Monday morning. But George had his very a good back four, back five if you include David Seaman as well and he knew he could win success on the back of that.
>
> Ray Parlour in conversation with the author.

> You generally felt the Cup Winners' Cup back then was looked on as the Europa League is looked upon now, something you just have to do. Until, I must stress, you get to the latter stages when the possibility of winning it makes it incredibly sexy. Which is basically what happened with Arsenal in 1993/94 I think.
>
> Patrick Barclay in conversation with the author.

Our discussion is going well. Alan Smith has relaxed to the point where we swap notes on our shorthand skills. I feel emboldened enough to ask him his memories of George Graham.

He thinks and then says,

> He was a hard task-masker. He was a manager who wanted to see your best and he wanted that every week and every day in training. He was always on the training pitch. He was a tracksuit manager. He was demanding, but the first-half of his tenure

we were winning things, and he was a happy man, but there would always be a bollocking every now and then even when we were doing really well.

I remember one game against Sheffield United just before Ian Wright signed for us. We beat them 5–2 but he gave us a right bollocking because I think we were 5–0 up at half-time but conceded two in the second-half! He was demanding, but he was great to play for. He was a striker himself so he used to take the forwards in training, teaching us to head the ball in training. He thought he was the best header of the ball in the club!

I think tactically he was very astute. When we got knocked out of the European Cup in 1991 by Benfica, by the time we got back into Europe for the 1993/94 European Cup Winners Cup run he made us harder to beat with 4-3-3, so he certainly learned from that defeat in 1991 to help us win in 1994.

I scored four against Austria Vienna in the first round in 1991 when we beat them 6–1 and we should have beaten Benfica too. Tony Adams had a chance close in and I had a chance to too. [With regret] We should have beaten them. They had the two Russian boys Isias and Yuran. [With a hint of a smile] They ended up at Millwall didn't they? That was a gutting night that was as we really should have won.

He took us all the way and got us to two finals on the trot. So tactically yes he was great. You all knew your job and you had to do your job within that system.

I then ask him 'what was it like to play with David Rocastle?' Immediately, and with great fondness, he replies,

He was a special lad. And he was a special talent. My wife and me went to an end-of-season dinner at the Grosvenor Hotel and Rocky, who was about eighteen at the time, came across and introduced himself and said, 'If there's anything you need, just let me know'. As a teenager, that behaviour was quite unusual to see so we immediately thought, 'Well, he's a nice lad'. And that was the first time we met him. He became a very close friend.

As a player he was spectacular. You don't see many these days who had the talent he did, the technique – but who can mix it. It was sad to see the talent he had, not go to waste – but he had a knee operation they messed up which restricted his mobility after that, and he put on a bit of weight, and it became difficult for him after that. As a player he had the skills of a Brazilian and the fighting spirit of a German. You'd get players trying to intimidate him but he'd come in at half-time and be laughing about it. Stuart Pearce and him always had a running battle but deep down Pearcey knew he couldn't get the better of him. He knew Rocky wasn't only greatly talented but he loved a fight in terms of the one-on-one battle you get between players – but also because Pearce knew Rocky was tough – and loved a fight.

What typified him was when he won that free kick at Anfield. He got up with a clenched fist and clenched teeth and said, 'Come on lads we can do this'. He was a marvellous player. And as a lad [trails off]. You know it's still hard to talk about it. We still keep in touch with his family even now …

Alan Smith looks genuinely distraught at the mention of David Rocastle's name. It is testament to Smith's emotional intelligence and sensitivity that recalling the first-class human being David 'Rocky' Rocastle was still projects such a raw and humane reaction.

It is also of course tribute to what an exceptional person Rocky was, and always will be, in the minds of so many. I wrote a tribute piece on him for the website *Sabotage Times*, run by former *Loaded* editor James Brown, on the twelfth anniversary of his tragic death. It was humbling to read so many Arsenal fans post their memories of him, but what also struck me was the fact that Leeds United, Manchester City, Norwich City and Hull City fans also got in touch to share their positive recollections of him.

He left a mark on everyone he met. As an Arsenal man that makes me so proud. He would surely have made a mark on the 1993/94 Gunners side too, if it hadn't been for the frustrating knee injuries that curtailed his career.

When George Graham broke the news to him that he was being sold in the summer of 1992 to Leeds United, Rocky said he was so numb at leaving his beloved club he simply sat in his car and broke down in tears. No wonder Alan Smith told me Rocky was a special lad.

Sensing that Smith would like to move the conversation on I try and change the tone to a more light-hearted one. I say to him,

> Ahead of the European Cup Winners' Cup competition Arsenal qualified by winning the FA Cup in 1993. I've got to ask you is it true you went up to the ref in the 1993 FA Cup Final replay and said in your loudest Brummie accent – just as he was about to book you for the first and only time in your footballing career – 'Referee. Are you aware of my excellent disciplinary record?'

Alan smiles and replies dryly,

> Gary Lineker tells the story I said that in a Leicester game but I didn't! It was such a stupid booking though. The booking letter from the FA is in a frame at home though. It was for the delaying of the taking of a free kick. I did have it on the wall in my study but I took it down. [Dryly] I'll have to put it up again.
>
> I'd never go through my career with only one booking if I was playing now. No chance. Not the way I played. I used my elbows to jump and you'd get more refs pulling you up for that now. I remember cutting big Steve Foster on the head, even though he used to wear those big white headbands. I caught him and he'd gone off to have five stiches. He thought I'd did it on purpose, 'I'm going to have you'. But I really didn't mean to.

I interviewed Ray Parlour for the *London Evening Standard* last year, and I also asked him about what George Graham was like. He told me,

George was fantastic. George was great. He was obviously a little bit different, he was more of a person who might have a go at you if you didn't play as well as you could. George had his own style of management whereas Arsene Wenger would look at the video and pull us aside on the Monday morning. But George had his very a good back four, back five if you include David Seaman as well and he knew he could win success on the back of that.

I think Arsene Wenger would always say that when he first came to Arsenal he was very lucky to have inherited such a good back five from George, great players who were capable of winning trophies. George was great to me as well. I obviously made my debut under George, so I owe him a lot for picking me.

Moving the conversation to a more European theme, I then asked Ray (who's a lovely bloke with an impish sense of humour and a ready smile, but with a keen football brain and great recall of Arsenal matches) what was more disappointing: Losing to Real Zaragoza in the 1995 European Cup Winners' Cup Final the year after The Miracle of Copenhagen, or losing to Galatasary in the UEFA Cup Final in 2000 when rioting broke out – in sharp contrast to the wonderful scenes of 1994 between Arsenal and Parma?

Ray, who was an unused substitute in Copenhagen replied,

If you look at Paris 1995 the year before when we won against Parma where we only had one shot on target, when Alan Smith scored with a shot from distance, you'd argue we rode our luck. So although losing the final to Zaragoza in 1995 was disappointing you could say we'd up our luck the year before in Copenhagen.

You're always disappointed when you lose any game but losing to Galatasaray was very disappointing. We had so many chances. [It finished 0-0 aet]. When it went to penalties I remember taking a penalty. Fortunately I scored – but the other lads missed! [They lost 4–1 on penalties. Ray was the only Arsenal player to score in the shootout]. Davor Suker missed. Patrick Vieira missed. It was disappointing. But it was tough taking those penalties because it was in front of the Galatasary fans. [At the Parken Stadium, Copenhagen]. They were very passionate fans, you know there were flares going off and everything so it was always going to be tough taking a penalty-shoot in front of them, you're always going to be disappointed losing a European final but Galatasary was a very big disappointment in my career. That season 1999/2000 was a great campaign for me, I think I played well all the way through and even scoring a hat-trick at Werder Bremen earlier in that run to the final so I would have to say Galatasary in 2000.

I then asked him whether he kept in touch with the Arsenal boys. He smiled and replied immediately, 'Yes I do. Tony Adams is probably still my best mate. [Chuckles conspiratorially] He taught me some bad habits!'

I reply, 'I shouldn't ask really should I?' He laughed and shot back good-naturedly, 'no!'

Ray Parlour was always an interesting player. As someone who was so obviously talented and imbued with great fitness levels and a tenacity often underestimated by opponents, he was in danger of not fulfilling his potential towards the end of George Graham's reign. He was certainly used sparingly in the whole of the 1993/94 season only really flourishing when he genuinely bought into Arsenal Wenger's new methods.

George Graham's first signing for Arsenal Perry Groves, who played from 1986–1992, also gave me an insight into the George Graham who was at the height of his powers and who used his experiences of the short-lived 1991 European Cup games to great effect in 1993/94.

In an interview for *The Gooner* in association with huge Arsenal fan Josh Landy's 'Play with a Legend' he told me,

> When I was twenty-one I was the top player in Colchester and I was a big fish in a small pond. But when George Graham signed me for Arsenal my first training session was something else. You go from being the top dog at Colchester to Arsenal to having to prove yourself in single every training session at Arsenal let alone during a match.
>
> The first game after I signed I watched was Arsenal v Spurs at Highbury. George Graham said you're not going to be in the first team today I want you to watch. And the pace, the passing, the thought processes, the decision making, it was at a different level. I was nervous but I was excited because it was another challenge. I could do a training session at Colchester at eighty per cent and knew I was going to play on the Saturday. But training at Arsenal when I first joined I'd be with players like Charlie Nicholas, Viv Anderson, Kenny Sansom, people I'd watched on TV. David Rocastle. What a player. I'd heard he was an up and coming talent but during training George Graham would have him and me taking corners and set pieces for hours on end at the near post driven in, or centred to the penalty spot.

As Groves had been moved on before the 1994 European Cup Winners' Cup success I ask him about the two best Arsenal teams he played in and how he'd compare the 1989 and 1991 title seasons and which was the better side, Groves responds,

> I'd say they both had different qualities. 1988/89 was very well structured, very well organised. Everybody knew their jobs, we were very disciplined. People said we were boring, we weren't. We had flair in David Rocastle who was great on the ball, industrious, a good tackler and creative. Paul Merson was creative, Paul Davis, who played in the 1994 Cup Winners' Cup Final in Copenhagen, was creative.
>
> But I think the 1991 side had a bit more arrogance, a bit more belief. There was a group of us, about seven or eight, who'd already won the league in 1989 and there was a difference in our mental attitude because we had belief, we knew we could win,

not hoped we could win. We knew we could win because we'd already had experience of winning. And that's so important.

Psychologically prior to 1989 Liverpool were dominant and everyone was really frightened of them. But when we played them in 1988/89 in the League Cup three times, 1–1 at Anfield, 0–0 at Highbury then we lost 2–1 at Villa Park that was really important in terms of performances. The thing was in that first game at Anfield we absolutely battered them. Rocky scored a brilliant goal and you could see some of the Liverpool players looking at each other and going, 'This team has come to Anfield and they think they can beat us'.

So that 1991 side was a great team. And signing Dave Seaman in the summer of 1991 gave us something more at the back. John Lukic was a very good keeper but Dave Seaman was a great keeper. And signing Anders gave us even more creativity. So that 1991 side had more arrogance, but in a nice way. I think the fans got that too. When teams used to turn up at Highbury in 1991 the fans had the feeling that we would win.

It was similar to the Invincibles, not that I'm trying to compare us to them, but when the 1991 side went 1–0 up you knew we would win, and the Invicibles had that too. You could see the other team thinking, 'There's no way we can score two'.

Perry had a good friendship with Tony Adams as part of the 'Tuesday Club.' Tony Adams is a very different person now and I was interested to find out whether Groves still had contact with The Gunners' defensive lynchpin who was so central to the success the side achieved in 1993/94.

It's like a band of brothers. You get a bond. Like me and Merse, and Nigel Winterburn and Alan Smith and so on. I try to explain it to people that it's like a band of brothers. The 2014 and 2015 teams will have that now. By winning the FA Cup they now have a place in Arsenal's history and they will have that forever. That's what we've been missing as a club. Aaron Ramsey, Jack Wilshere, Kieran Gibbs and so on, these current players now have a bond and the will have the bond for the rest of their lives just like the 1989 and 1991 sides I played have.

Perry is absolutely spot on in what he said. Every successful team is like a 'Band of Brothers'. Not everyone has to like each other in any team or in any workplace, you only have to look at the coldness between Teddy Sheringham and Andy Cole at Manchester United during their glory years to realise that. However there does have to be utter respect for the other person in terms of doing your best for them and every one of your teammates for the greater good.

And the Arsenal team of 1993/94 had that in spades.

As a freelancer at the *London Evening Standard* I've been lucky enough to talk to a mentor of mine about football, the great Patrick Barclay. A man who has covered nearly twenty international tournaments and seen every great team of the last fifty years who recalls the Arsenal side of 1993/94 for me.

It is always an education when I talk to the great man, he is as warm, gregarious and helpful as his copy is as original, sharp and insightful. As with much of his writing, a leitmotiv of his is to set the scene in a wider context.

When he spoke about 1993/94 he told me, 'It was interesting European football hadn't reached the levels it had now with wall-to-wall coverage, and British and English clubs taking on continental teams in competition very much played second fiddle to the domestic league'.

We speak the day after the 2015 Champions League winners Barcelona, and their ridiculously talented triumvirate of Lionel Messi, Neymar and Lusi Suarez utterly destroyed Pep Guardiola's Bayern Munich in the imposing Camp Nou with all the ensuing coverage and hyperbole. Patrick explains,

> There simply wasn't the tremendous excitement similar to last night. I was glued to the screen last night even though there was no British interest, and it wasn't like that twenty-one years ago I don't think.
>
> You generally felt the Cup Winners' Cup back then was looked on as the Europa League is looked upon now, something you just have to do. Until, I must stress you get to the latter stages, when the possibility of winning it makes it incredibly sexy. Which is basically what happened with Arsenal in 93/94 I think. [...] There was a very defensive mind-set employed at Arsenal around that time with the George Graham era about to go into decline – to the extent that by the end of his reign all that was left was the defensive excellence of the team. From 1991 the attacking force was nowhere near the same as it was prior to then.

Paddy is absolutely correct. At times watching Arsenal week in, week out during the 1993/94 season it did feel like defensive excellence was all we had left and even then domestically there were wobbles including the 3-1 defeat by Bolton Wanderers in the Fourth Round replay in front of 6,000 overjoyed travellers from the north west.

Defensive excellence in Europe was another matter entirely. And you could argue the defensive cover started in midfield with the excellent screening given by unsung players such as Ian Selley.

I ask Stewart Houston how important a player like Ian Selley was to the side that year:

> George and I gave Ian Selley a start against Odense. He was a small lad. There wasn't much strength there but he was a very technical player. He was a fit lad. He was an intelligent player. Neat and tidy. He'd a small frame, there wasn't too much of him but at that particular time we gave him his chance and he took it. No question about it.

Houston's perceptive comments about the unfortunate Selly were brought home by the fact he broke his leg against Leicester City at Highbury in February 1995, and was never the same player again.

They say when the legendary Joe Mercer broke his leg which ended his career you could hear the crack all around Highbury. I was there the day Selley broke his leg and for those of a certain vintage it was our Joe Mercer moment. I can still recall the awful sound of the crack reverberate around a stunned Highbury as the crowd immediately fell silent.

Stewart agrees, 'When he broke his leg in February 1995 it was a terrible shame for the lad'.

Momentarily we both fall silent thinking of the capriciousness of football and sport in general, where one minute you can be lifting a European trophy with friends and teammates, the whole of your career to look forward to, the next, in a blink of an eye (and the awful snap of a bone) you're washed up and finished in professional football.

Before the silence gets too long I ask, 'Were you worried at any stage during the 1-1 home-leg draw against Odense at Highbury?'

Stewart replies,

In those days the away goals were always in the back of your mind. You try not to let it affect you but it does get into your mind at times and despite not letting it affect you, it does to a certain extent. Of course it's still around in the modern day in the knock out stages of the Champions League, for example when Arsenal got knocked out by Monaco on away goals in March 2015.

It's always lying there, and it's a concern but the most important thing is to win a football match.

And if not win, make deadly sure you're in the hat for the next round by not losing. Which is what Arsenal did in that second-leg at home to Odense.

The consistently excellent journalist Steve Tongue gave me his views on Odense and George Graham ahead of the 2015 FA Cup Final (which Arsenal memorably won 4–0 against an insipid Aston Villa side) led by the former Spurs manager (and alleged huge Gooner) Tim Sherwood.

In fact the 2015 4–0 win against Villa was probably the most one sided FA Cup Final since Manchester United eclipsed a pre-Abramovich Chelsea 4–0 days before The Miracle of Copenhagen occurred.

The likeable journo who is currently writing a book on David Beckham to be published by Amberley said,

I'd always got on well with George Graham since the time he was manager of Millwall, when I was the ghost writer for his programme notes. In 1993–94 I was working for Radio 5 and saw Arsenal about twenty times that season, including several of the European games.

The Cup-Winners' Cup could be a funny competition, in that some European countries where the domestic cup wasn't taken too seriously could come up with a pretty small team as their representative, whereas others (like England) were quite likely to have some heavy-hitters.

Odense were a reasonable Danish club at the time, though you'd probably have expected Arsenal to come through a bit more comfortably than they did.

Indeed. The return game at Highbury saw an organised Odense team stifle any plans Arsenal had to turn the match into a goal glut. Goalless at half-time, Kevin Campbell allayed any nerves the home crowd had with a goal in the fifty-second minute.

The fact Allan Nielsen enabled the travelling Danes to reach parity on the night with an equaliser four minutes from time only added to the sense that the Gunners were becoming increasingly nervous at the thought their opponents were going to take the tie to the uncertainty of extra-time.

However, the home side prevailed, and if the 1-1 draw on the night completed a winning, if underwhelming 3-2 victory on aggregate. The fact was that the north Londoners were through to the second round and ultimately another trip to Denmark. A far more auspicious trip.

As the *Guardian* headline the next morning said, 'Arsenal Escape'. And if there was more space in the two deck shape they would surely have added 'and Live to Fight Another Day.'

3

Arsenal vs Standard Liège: The Emperor's New Clothes

European Cup Winners' Cup, second round, first-leg. 20 October 1993. Arsenal 3 Standard Liège 0.

> Enjoy life. There's plenty of time to be dead.
>
> Hans Christian Andersen.

> I think British clubs all play the same style. Arsenal should know that my players are used to it and are not afraid of anyone. It's an advantage my team has played British sides before. The English way of playing isn't my favourite. I prefer to watch French and German football on TV instead.
>
> Arie Haan, Standard Liège manager.

> That first match against Liège … I don't think we were thinking about winning the tournament then. I think we were just excited about being in it.
>
> Amy Lawrence.

On the first day of school in September 1898, the pupils of Collège Saint-Servais in Liège started a football club called Standard of Liège. Standard, whose official name is Royal Standard Club of Liège settled in Sclessin, an industrial area of Liège in 1909. Similar to Arsenal the club gained promotion back to the top division in 1921 and has never been relegated since.

The club has a European pedigree as well as a domestic one. In the 1960s the club reached the semi-finals of the European Cup in 1961/62, only losing to eventual runners-up Real Madrid 0-6 on aggregate. They reached the same stage of the European Cup Winners' Cup in 1966/67 before losing to eventual champions Bayern Munich. In the 1960s and early 1970s Standard won six Belgian First Division titles, two Belgian Cups and a League Cup.

Managed by the wily Austrian Ernst Happel, Standard won the Belgian Cup again in 1981. The following year, Raymond Goethals took control of the team. Led by

'Raymond Science' the club was twice the champions of Belgium, as well as two-time victors of the Belgian Supercup, also reaching the final of the European Cup Winners' Cup in 1982 where they played the mighty Barcelona at their home ground unsurprisingly losing 2-1. So when, on 6 June 1993, Standard won the Belgian Cup for the fifth time in their history, eclipsing Charleroi at the Constant Vanden Stock Stadium in Brussels to take their place in the European Cup Winners' Cup competition at the start of 1993/94 every Arsenal fan was aware of them in the draw.

Before the first-leg at Highbury Liège manager Arie Haan, a classy midfielder who played in the 'Total Football' Ajax and Dutch sides of the seventies, told the media somewhat dammingly, 'I think British clubs all play the same style. Arsenal should know that my players are used to it and are not afraid of anyone. It's an advantage my team has played British sides before.' He was correct about that, and the fact that Liège had beaten three British sides. But he was running down Arsenal Football Club if he thought we were at the same level as Portadown, Hearts and Cardiff City.

He continued his mind-games (or was it simply him being unnecessarily denigrating?) when he declared with withering arrogance, 'The English way of playing isn't my favourite. I prefer to watch French and German football on TV instead.'

George Graham, speaking to the press the day before the match explained portentously, 'A below-par performance in Europe usually means you are knocked out straight away'. At the end of the first leg George was right. Except it wasn't Arsenal who had to worry, it was Haan and his shell-shocked team.

I ask Stewart Houston what he remembers of that first leg match. He replies, 'I remember Paul Merson scoring with a free kick in the 3-0 win against Standard Liège in the second round. I recall the tie. It was an amazing couple of games especially the away one of course.'

Houston has somewhat unfairly been criticised for his tactical nous. But when I talked to him he was extremely articulate at explaining the tactics Arsenal played that night and through the course of the European run. He didn't overcomplicate it, but at the same time it was crystal clear to me that he knew what he was talking about, and his grasp and understanding (not to mention why the tactics were employed to such effect) were first rate. It was my abiding memory of him. The fact that his tactical insights were superb. He explained,

With our 4-3-3 formation we tended to play with three men up front, but they were all centre-forwards, interchanging between Kevin Campbell, Paul Merson, Ian Wright and Alan Smith, although Wrighty was rested for Liège away as he was on a booking as I remember.

The point is they weren't wingers. They were forwards who could score goals who played out wide in a front three which was the magic of it. The two 'wingers' in our front three were wide-men not wingers. They were forwards who played out wide and that was a crucial difference. It helped us in that run certainly because they could provide important goals too, not just crosses.

With our centre-forward roaming across the box, if the ball was played into on the right side, our left sided wide-man could get in the box and behave as another centre forward to trouble the opposition. If it was Campbell, playing as a wide-man, who was in the box he immediately became a second striker rather than a winger who happened to be in the box. He certainly wasn't standing on the opposite wing looking at what was happening in the box, he immediately became a second striker. And it worked. It certainly confused a lot of teams.

Confused teams it did. None more so than the complacent and poor Liège side over both legs of that tie. But Liège were poor because Arsenal were stunning over the course of 180 minutes in that glorious match up. Alan Smith recalls his experience of the tie and of European defenders and tactics,

Yes Standard Liège was an easy game for us, an easy tie for us, just as Austria, Vienna was in the European Cup in 1991 but there were a lot of difficult challenges and difficult teams we played in the cup run of 1993/94 and the year after.

Defenders would mark you differently, there would be more man on man, they would mark you that little bit tighter. There would be different tricks you would face in Europe compared to in the league.

The journalist and broadcaster Amy Lawrence put an original slant on proceedings when she spoke to me on the 26th anniversary of Anfield 1989. She told me,

I think it's really interesting reflecting on what Europe meant then from today's perspective because nowadays Arsenal qualifying for the Champions League is normal. So from that standpoint it's really quite odd to look back and think European football – even the competition once considered the third most important competition in Europe, and which became defunct – was monumental. People underestimate and sometimes mock the Europa League, certainly in England. However back then the European Cup Winners' Cup was supposedly the next one down from that, but all three were hugely respected.

The other significant thing was that people forget is the fact that Arsenal were denied a shot at the European Cup in 1989. Post Heysel in 1985 English clubs were banned from competing in Europe. So if we bear in mind Arsenal's 1991 experience was quite short lived (they only played Vienna and Benfica) so you're talking about the club playing four European games in a decade over a period of a month in 1991.

In 1993/94 European football was a nirvana that Arsenal fans were not used to tasting. Therefore to get back into Europe was very exciting. There were a lot of fans who were desperate to go on European trips. European football was still a little bit dangerous. I'm not saying it's completely and absolutely guaranteed to be safe and secure now but certainly in those days there was a consciousness that if you went overseas there might be a bit of bother. I can certainly remember being tear gassed in Italy around that time. I can't recall whether it was Sampdoria in the European Cup Winners' Cup of 1995 or whether it was in Torino during that cup run of 1994. However I do remember being chased, not individually but with my little group by a very unsavoury group of characters in Vienna in 1991, and being far more frightened than I dared to admit at the time.

I think there were six of us. One bloke at the front who had an umbrella, and one guy at the back who took some photographs who had a tripod and the ones who were far less experienced, or far less aware of how to behave on European trips were in the middle sort of trying not to catch anyone's eye and making a break for the station!

It was slightly different times to what we consider to be more normal these days. So I just think the overall context of being in Europe and travelling to the continent for European games was different. Also as a supporter you were representing your club in a way that felt more different than to now. As European football was on every week but now every game is accessible at the press of a button, you can live almost anywhere and have different knowledge of different teams and different players and different characteristics of different clubs. But that clearly wasn't the case in the early 1990s, particularly after the ban of English clubs. You felt like you were representing English clubs as a supporter when you travelled in those days.

You don't need to walk into a bar in some far flung place now and tell them about the Arsenal team because people know about the club and the team through the exposure of football and Arsenal and English fans know all about overseas teams for the same reason.

During that first match against Liège I don't think we were thinking about winning the tournament at the start of the season. I think we were just excited about being in it. It was a good draw to start with. To borrow a footballing cliché it really was just taking one round and one match at a time because I don't think anybody actually thought about winning it, or would even think that far ahead back then.

Amy was correct about taking one match at time, for the fans as well as players, there was still some apprehension over the second leg despite the comprehensive dismantling of Standard Liège 3-0.

A happy George Graham said after the game 'I was delighted by the performance,' adding mischievously, 'It's not often I can say that'. If he was happy at a 3-0 win he was in for another shock in Belgium in the return leg two weeks later.

The shell-shocked but still arrogant Haan added bitterly, 'Arsenal had more quality than us but the team with more quality doesn't always win. The tie is not finished yet.' By the end of the second leg he'd realise how utterly wrong he was in saying such arrant nonsense as Arsenal produced one of the greatest results and performances in its entire history.

Arsene Wenger's Monaco secured a vital 0–0 at Spartak Moscow, which was more to do with the spirit and effort of one player in particular, Gilles Grimandi.

L'Equipe, October, 21, 1993.

Arsenal's Ian Wright (on his knees) is hugged by teammates after he scored against Paris St Germain during the first period of their European Cup Winners' Cup semi-final first leg match on Tuesday 29 March 1994 in Paris. The final score was a 1-1 draw. (AP Photo/Laurent Rebours)

Above: Steve Ashford's great pal, the late Dave Wingate in Copenhagen: 'They did it for me Steve.'

Below: Outside the Stadio Delle Alpi.

Above: Before away-match tickets all looked the same.

Right: The moment the author and his friends realised 'that woman's a bloke!'

Left to right, Arsenal's Brian Marwood, Steve Bould, David Seaman, Paul Merson and Nigel Winterburn train before the match.

The «Gunners» story...

Notre retour en Europe s'assimile à un vaste tour des îles britanniques. Mise à part une incursion en terre bour guignonne, nos devoirs européens nous conduisent invariablement outre Channel.

Après Portadown, Hearts of Midlothian et Cardiff City, le tirage au sort nous offre Arsenal, une noix infiniment plu dure à croquer que les phalanges précitées.

Un bref retour dans le passé nous permet de nous souvenir. Le Standard écrivit quelques pages parmi les plu belles de son histoire européenne face à des équipes britanniques. Hearts of Midlothian constitue notre premièr expérience en Coupe d'Europe, c'était en 1958 (qualif. 5-1, 1-2). En février 1962, nous tombions sur les Rangers d Glasgow en 1/4 de finale de la Coupe des Champions. Leeds United et Liverpool constituent autant de défaites mai nos joueurs tombèrent la tête haute et les armes à la main face à des équipes alors au sommet de leur art.

Le football insulaire nous rend une fois de plus visite et, quel que soit le résultat de ce soir, Standard-Arsenal constitue une grande affiche. Nous pensons que le résultat du match aller n'hypothéquera en rien le spectacle de ce soir. Il n'entre pas dans les habitudes des équipes britanniques de vivre sur leur avance, des traditions solidement établies prouvent que le Standard ne refuse jamais le combat.

Un peu d'histoire

Arsenal vit le jour en 1886 sous le nom de Dial Square F.C. Le Club fut fondé par des ouvriers d'une fabrique de munition et hérita du surnom de «Gunners», il fixait ses pénates à Woolwich dans le Sud de Londres. Un des fondateurs, Fred Beardsley avait milité sous les couleurs de Nottingham Forest. Il se tourna tout naturellement vers son ancien club qui lui envoya un ballon et des vareuses rouges. Les Woolwich Reds étaient nés. Arsenal est toujours resté fidèle aux couleurs de ses débuts. Le nom du Club fut plusieurs fois modifié: Royal Arsenal, Woolwich Arsenal. Il devenait l'Arsenal Football Club peu avant la Seconde Guerre mondiale. Cette nouvelle appellation coïncide avec le déménagement à Highbury.

Highbury, haut lieu du foot anglais, curieux mélange de modernisme et de charme un peu rétro. En effet, la tribune sud fut complètement rénovée et la North Stand tribune comporte 53 loges. Les deux tribunes latérales, construites dans les années trente, n'ont pas été modifiées donnant ainsi à l'ensemble un cachet typique et oh combien chaleureux. Fouler la pelouse de Highbury ne constitue pas un moindre affaire, l'ambiance y est tou jours assurée. Nos joueurs peuvent e témoigner.

Une victoire par le plus petit écart es aujourd'hui encore qualifiée de «scor Arsenal». Mais d'où vient donc cett expression désormais célèbre? Dan les années trente, Arsenal accumula les succès (5 titres, 2 coupes) mais so style ne laissait place qu'à deux atta quants ne déchaînait pas la passio des adeptes du style offensif générale ment prôné en Grande-Bretagne. Le Reds inscrivaient un but et leu défense faisait le reste.

Un adversaire coriace

Arsenal, on s'en doute, n'en est pas sa première expérience européenn La vitrine aux trophées des Lond

Misplaced optimism in the Standard Liège vs Arsenal match programme.

Wright, attaquant.

George Graham, entraîneur.

Fondation: 1886.

Entraîneur: George Graham.

Stade: Highbury (48.000 places)

Face aux clubs belges
Eliminé par le F.C. Liège en C3 (2e tour) en 1963-1964 (1-1, 1-3).
Victoire contre Anderlecht en C3 (finale) en 1969-1970 (1-3, 3-0).
Victoire contre Beveren en C3 (3e tour) en 1970-1971 (4-0, 0-0)
Eliminé par Winterslag en C3 (2e tour) en 1981-1982 (0-1, 2-0)

Palmarès
Champion d'Angleterre en 1931, 1933, 1934, 1935, 1938, 1948, 1953, 1971, 1989, 1991.

Coupe d'Angleterre en 1930, 1936, 1950, 1971, 1989, 1991, 1993.

League Cup en 1987 et 1993.

Coupe des Villes de Foire en 1970.

Les records
En championnat:
Meilleur résultat: 12-0 contre Loughborough en 1900.
Défaite: 0-8 contre Loughborough en 1896.
Plus grand nombre de points: 83 en 1990-1991 (division 1).
Buts inscrits: 127 en 1930-1931 (division 1).
Meilleur buteur: Ted Drake, 42 buts en 1934-1935.
Meilleur buteur en carrière: Cliff Bastin, 150 buts de 1930 à 1947.
Joueur le plus capé: Kenny Sansom, 86 sélections pour l'Angleterre.
Record de sélections en équipe A: David O'Leary: 558 de 1975 à 1993.
Record pour un transfert: £2.000.000 pour David Rocastle transféré vers Leeds United, £1.300.000 pour David Seaman en provenance de Q.P.R. (1990).
En Coupe:
Plus grande victoire: 11-1 contre Darwen en 1932.

Les noyaux
Les deux entraîneurs effectueront leur choix parmi les joueurs suivants:
Arsenal: Seaman, Dixon, Adams, Bould, Winterburn, Davis, Jensen, Merson, Limpar, Smith, Wright, Keown, Linighan, Parlour, Heaney, Selley, Miller et Campbell.

Standard: Munaron, Nuyens, Genaux, Cruz, Léonard, Hellers, Pister, Van Rooy, Soudan, Rednic, Dinga, Smeets, Wilmots, Goossens, Asselman, Rychkov.

Arbitre: M. Kaj Natri assité de MM. Tapio Vli-Karro et Kari Koskela.
4e arbitre officiel: M. Juha Hirviniemi.

ens s'orne, entre autres, d'une Coupe
s Villes des Foires conquise en 1970
ce à Anderlecht. Soulignons encore
e les Gunners perdirent la Coupe
s Coupes en 1980 face à Valence.
tte année, les Anglais éliminèrent
lense au premier tour (2-1, 1-1).

rès avoir réussi un impressionnant
ublé en 1971 (Championnat et Cup),
s «Gunners» campent au sommet de
hiérarchie anglaise depuis la moitié
s années quatre-vingt. Leur carte de
te s'orne de quelques morceaux
nthologie: League Cup en 1987 et
93, Coupe d'Angleterre en 1993, F.A.
p en 1989, 1991 et 1993, titre natio-
en 1989 et 1991. Chacun a encore
mémoire la finale de la dernière Cup
Wembley. Le replay face à Sheffield
dnesday constitue un modèle du
re, Andy Linighan n'inscrivit le but
la victoire qu'à une minute de la fin
l'ultime prolongation. Il déposait
si le trophée le plus prestigieux pour
anglais dans les mains de son
ager, George Graham.

nqueur comme joueur de la League
en 1965, sous les couleurs de
lsea, Graham est impliqué dans
s les succès d'Arsenal lors de la
ière décennie. Graham est le seul
ais à avoir remporté tous les tro-
es comme joueur ou comme
ager.

e accumulation de succès lui
ne sans conteste le titre de numéro
Anglais de ces dix dernières
es.

nal c'est aussi Ian Wright. Treize

fois international, la perle noire de Highbury s'avère être la meilleure gâchette des «Gunners» (15 roses en championnat, 15 en Coca Cola Cup, 10 en F.A. Cup. Les autres forwards londoniens (Alan Smith, Merson et Campbell) sont beaucoup moins performants. Au fait Arsenal manque cruellement d'efficacité en zone de conclusion.

Commandé par le gardien Seaman, le bastion défensif constitue le point fort des «Red and White». Arsenal compte en outre en ses rangs plusieurs étrangers de valeur: les avants Anders Limpar (international suédois) et Steve Morrow (Irlande du Nord), le demi John Jensen (international danois) et l'arrière Eddie McGoldrick (Irlande). L'effectif des «Gunners» s'agrémente aussi de plusieurs internationaux britanniques: le gardien David Seaman, les défenseurs Lee Dixon, Tony Adams, Martin Keown et Nigel Winterburn, les avants Ian Wright, Paul Merson et Alan Smith.

Il existe donc un certain déséquilibre entre les secteurs défensifs et offensifs. Il est pourtant certain que les grosses pointures défensives peuvent compenser la carence des forwards anglais. Il suffit pour s'en convaincre de parcourir les classements de la très exigeante première league, Arsenal se situe au second rang derrière Manchester United. Quand nous vous disions que nous allions vivre une très grande soirée européenne...

Above: On the coach from Milan to Turin.

Below: Copenhagen's city centre full of Gooners

4

Standard Liège vs Arsenal: The Tinderbox

European Cup Winners' Cup, second round, second-leg. 3 November 1993. Standard Liège 0 Arsenal 7 (Arsenal win 10-0 on aggregate).

Travelling expands the mind rarely.

Hans Christian Andersen.

Alas, fate turned its back on us in the first-leg in London. Standard came upon the best possible Arsenal. […] We can always dream. In football, so many things can happen […] More than ever and above all in adversity let us have confidence in our players!
Standard Liège club president Jean Wauters quoted in the match programme before the game.

I've been legged half-way around your fucking town, been fired at with water cannon, been herded onto a train that's going to Ostend for you to deport us for no reason and my bloody car's parked in the centre of Liège.
Battered and bruised Arsenal fan to Belgian riot police after the game.

Yes. But has anyone got any serious problems?
The response from a Belgian riot policeman.

The city of Liège is part of the Walloon, the French-speaking region of Belgium. It is situated in the valley of the Meuse River, in the east of the country, a short drive to the borders of the Netherlands and Germany. At Liège the Meuse River meets the river Ourthe which slices through the city.

Liège is also part of the *sillon industrie*, the former industrial backbone of Wallonia bursting with steel manufacturers, a Belgian equivalent of Sheffield. People in the town are renowned for their toughnesss. Not for nothing in the French language the city has the epithet *la cité ardente* (the fervent city). But in November 1993 this proud town was suffering from an industrial recession. As for its football team after an explosive 90 minutes from a rampant Arsenal team who gave a performance virtually unheard of in the latter part of George Graham's reign it too suffered in its own way.

In Newcastle three bone idle students were playing up to the stereotype by sitting around smoking in a shabby student house surrounded by the detritus of late night takeaways, empty lager cans, stolen road signs, peeling paintwork and fraying carpets. Through the alcohol, the talk turned to their beloved Arsenal. The three young lads barely out of their teens, and struggling to survive on a pittance, worked hard during breaks to fund their season tickets. In fact two of them had recently spent a summer picking grapes in deepest France just so they could have a few pennies to rub together, with the other moving from London to the south coast to earn as much as he could labouring.

No. 14 Simonside Terrace, Heaton was a place full of adventures yet to be lived or in some cases never to be lived. A place where impeccable idealism, unworkable ideas and unrealistic dreams co-mingled with hangovers and late nights. Where a set of young lads, including three Gooners, were trying to find their way in a life that was to prove far tougher to some than to others. 'I can't believe we beat Standard Liège 3-0 in the first-leg' said Arsenal fan number one, eyes glassy from the lager. At that point the unimaginable dream of the Dutch god that was Dennis Bergkamp (and Stefan Swartz's Arsenal Goujons) was still more than eighteen months away.

Through the twisting smoke and thudding, relentless beat of 'Wrote For Luck', Arsenal fan number two added, 'Yeah. Great result. Merse played a blinder at Highbury.' Arsenal fan number three added, 'Let's go and watch the second-leg'.

'Bet it won't be on in the pubs in town.' Replied Arsenal fan number two.

'No,' explained Arsenal fan number three suddenly becoming animated. 'Let's go and watch the game. Let's go to the away-leg in Liège.' No one knows how long it took to get an answer, whether it was an instant or whether it was another sixteen plays of 'Wrote for Luck', but eventually after much deliberation both of them replied in splendid unison, 'okay, let's go to Liège to watch Arsenal'.

All three delved deep into their thoughts about the club they loved unaware the trip they unexpected were about to go on would be remembered for the rest of their lives. Good friend and father of three Guy Wiseman from Hitchin, Herts, was one of those twenty-one-year-old students. He recalled fondly,

Going away to Belgium to finally watch Arsenal in Europe felt like the final frontier for a hardened away fan. After witnessing some classic away victories at Anfield, Old Trafford, Elland Road and White Hart Lane, the continent was all that was waiting to be ticked off the map. But in many ways it was just the beginning. The first of many fantastic European tours over the next ten years that propelled Arsenal into European elite from the shadows of the post-Heysel ban on English clubs in Europe. Fitting then that rather than rather than jumping into the glamour of the San Siro or Benfica's

Stadium of Light a year earlier, we chose the gritty industrial wasteland of Belgium as our first destination.

On reflection, the venue was a home from home for me as we set off at nightfall from Middlesbrough where I was studying at uni at the time. My two pals, Layth and Matt joined me from Newcastle where they were studying. There was just enough time to run some clippers through our hair for an ill thought through head shave, but unfortunately not enough time to recharge the clippers' battery to finish off the Matt's skull, leaving him with an amusing mullet for the trip.

We headed for the cross channel ferry before driving through the night to Brussels. The excitement was huge and as was the pattern of our behaviour at the time, we didn't wait until match-day to start the beers flowing. During a break from driving I lost my irreplaceable half Arsenal, half union jack hat while singing out of the window.

After finally finding the Atomium in Brussels we parked up and slept in the car as the sun rose. It was only Tuesday so we had plenty of time to plan some sightseeing and drove out on to Waterloo.

The walk up the Mount of the Lion provided our only element of healthy exercise and it seemed somehow fitting to visit the site. The huge statue of a Lion atop the mound even appeared to have its front foot resting on a football! As the visitor centre's leaflet proclaimed 'On 18 June 1815, the allied troops under the command of the Duke of Wellington and Marshall Blücher clashed with the army of the Emperor Napoleon some 18 miles from Brussels. The battle of Waterloo would seal the fate of Europe.' Little did we know that Eddie McGoldrick would seal Standard's fate the following evening!

That night we found a cheap B&B in Charleroi, seven years before the town played host to England's last game of Euro 2000, courtesy of a rash Phil Neville challenge versus Romania. The only thing of note from the Charleroi that night was the Cardiff City graffiti on a bus stop left by Welsh fans who had caused a few problems before getting knocked out of the same tournament by Standard Liège in the last round. Their legacy was also illustrated by the nervous police dog handler and his Alsatian who were the only other visitors to the soulless neon lit bar that we drank in that night. After staring at us for all of 25 mls of Juliper beer, they left understanding that the only harm we posed was to ourselves.

The Gooner editor Kevin Whitcher also recalls the trip with a huge amount of fondness.
He told me,

The second round saw the first-leg at home, against Belgians Standard Liège. A 3–0 home win made the second-leg a formality, but I and three pals has already made arrangements to travel to Belgium, as one of my cohorts, Dave, had a mate called Christian in Belgium he used to trade bootleg tapes with, and had visited to catch some gigs in the past.

Christian had bought us plum seats in the upper tier pitch-side in among the home fans. The journey was made in spite of a feeling that the tie was resolved. We went to a gig with Christian the night before the game to see Teenage Fanclub, and on the day of the game, we were pretty cautious as the police were expecting trouble. This was not too long after English clubs had been readmitted to UEFA competitions. There was a cordon a fair distance from the ground stopping people bringing in weapons, although we had parked within it before it was operational.

Rather amusingly, a local petrol station was giving away pint glasses with their petrol as some kind or promotion, effectively tooling up anyone who was within the cordon. The match itself was a procession, a 7-0 win for Arsenal including the rarity of an Eddie McGoldrick goal. Joyous as we were, on exiting the ground we decided, for reasons of self-preservation, on a policy of keeping our mouths shut until we got into the car, at which point we let out an ecstatic cheer.

Publisher Mike Francis, also of *The Gooner* added with a smile,

Kevin Whitcher, who would later take over from me as editor, recounted his drive to Liège in what he described as 'a Ford Cortina of some vintage' along with fellow *Gooner* contributors Dave, Warren and Mike. Kevin made no secret of the fact that the trip was a good excuse to stock up on duty-free beers for the winter, but was delighted to be in the ground to see the team score seven in a game, a feat he described as crossing the borders of reality and one he questioned whether he'd see again in his lifetime. Oh ye of little faith Kevin!

Former *Sky News* journalist Jem Maidment also recalls the trip with a great amount of affection,

What a game, what a night. People may forget that we were actually quite worried about meeting Standard when the teams were drawn together, there was definite trepidation before we beat them 3-0 at Highbury. Big name, well they were at the time, and we thought it would be tight.

So to win 10-0 on aggregate was something else, particularly 7-0 away when I don't think Ian Wright even played. Even Eddie McGoldrick scored for goodness sake. My abiding memory of the away game was being under the decrepit wooden away-end before the game and watching all these Arsenal fans ordering beers and getting drunk and raucous. I thought the beer tasted awful and when I asked a steward what it was he laughed and said it was non-alcoholic, which made sense. So all these Gooners were getting drunk on children's beer. It was no more potent than a can of Fanta! Oh, and I am pretty sure the home support had a bit of a lunatic fringe because when it got to about 4-0 they started fighting among themselves. Surreal. Standard were lucky to get Nil.

We got back the following more to Highbury with some great back pages to read but the ones I remember were all about Man United getting knocked out of the

Champions League at Galatasaray. It was the game when it all kicked off and Turkish police were hitting United players and Cantona went mad. [*The Guardian* headline the next morning read, 'Lacklustre United Punished in Hell'] It just made the night perfect, to be honest.

The match itself was simply unbelievable for Arsenal fans. Yet to be a travelling fan at your first away match in Europe took the sense of amazement to another level. From the teams point of view I asked Stewart Houston breathlessly, 'My first ever European away game at the tender age of twenty-one was at Liège. My pals and I had a ball in Belgium and I remember thinking surely it's not like this all the time?! Did you feel something similar?'

He replied,

It was an onslaught. It was one of the best performances I've ever been involved in both domestically and in Europe. It has to be one of the best European performances in Arsenal's history, not just the time we were there.

No disrespect to Liège they weren't a bad side either, [with pride] but we just ran riot that night. Once we got a couple of goals before we knew it, it was three, four, five, and then six and seven. It was just incredible. We took the game to them. We had a lot of momentum and when we got a couple of goals they lost a bit of heart and we just kept going at them we were relentless in that respect. It was an outstanding performance.

If you looked at that result you would have thought, 'Crikey what happened there, that's a good result from Arsenal'. And in a way that marked us out as a team that weren't simply there to make up the numbers. And it may have helped a little further down the line in terms of the teams we faced. The fact they knew we were capable of attacking to such devastating effect and weren't just a team who could defend very well.

It was just a very outstanding performance from the whole team.

As someone who was there with two friends I had to ask Stewart whether he was conscious of the tremendous away support that night.

He replied immediately and without hesitation,

We were always very attentive to our tremendous away following. There was a bond there, I'm not saying there isn't nowadays because there is but for me I remember there were times on that run when we could hear the fans and see the fans and all their flags and banners and what have you and it would raise the team. There are moments in any match when the team raises the fans and there are moments when the fans raise the team and that certainly happened all throughout that run. It's a combination of the two during ninety minutes. Of course sometimes the fans were quiet like any team but at other times they were very loud and supportive.

We always used to say to the players, not just during that run but domestically too, 'if you do your best then that's all you can do, just have a go'. So even if you're having a stinker or it's not happening for you on the night just have a go and the fans will always respect that and be on your side. Fans can sense it – always.

Nigel Maitland, an Arsenal regular since the late sixties and one of Arsenal's most loyal and long-serving season ticket holders went to every game on that run bar Odense away.

The London taxi driver, story teller supreme and good friend of mine told me,

What do I remember about Standard Liège away? Blimey, I'll give you some brief and blurred memories. For Liège, me, Micky and Dave Lillywhite got into Paul's car after a 'couple' of pints and headed for Dover the night before the game. On the way we saw a signpost for a place called Thong and thought we really should have a drink in somewhere with such a stupid name. After that it became a sort of game that we had to stop at anywhere with a silly name. My favourite was Nackington but you wouldn't believe how many ridiculously named villages, hamlets, and towns there are in Kent. Suffice to say, it took us a tad longer to get to Dover than had been planned. Paul, as ever, was very patient. When we got to Dover he arranged a discounted ferry fare with the Arsenal supporting ticketing officer and the next thing we knew we were waking up, it was daylight and we were hurtling through the Belgian countryside towards Liège.

Upon arrival we parked up and our day took a turn for the worse. Apparently Cardiff had ripped the place to pieces in an earlier round and by the look of the mass ranks of riot police lightening was not about to strike twice. Additionally we had not booked a hotel as it was pre-internet days wasn't it? So everywhere was fully booked although we got the impression this was on the orders of the local plod.

We did what any self-respecting away fan would do and headed straight for the smallest, crappiest bar we could find to consider our options and wait for Ollie and Mark who were coming by motorbike and also had the tickets. After a few hours Paul found out that there was a hotel about an hour's drive away (a Holiday Inn I think) with vacancies. Mick and I had young children at the time so the thought of stopping drinking at any stage when we had been given a 'pass' was not an option so we volunteered to wait in the bar for Ollie and Mark. Needed to make sure we got the tickets see!

The rest of the afternoon was a bit of a blur, as usual, but I remember playing darts with one of the locals who celebrated like he'd won at Ally Pally when he beat me. I later found out that he had been playing for years in the bar after insisting that they put a dartboard in and I was the first person to actually lose to him.

I think Ollie lived in France at the time which is probably why we had tickets in Liège's main stand. As we were 3–0 up from the first-leg the game was probably a formality anyway but a few early goals put the tie to rest. Micky, whose small grasp of French/Belgian had been pissed down the bar's urinals, took great pleasure in screaming, 'Sortie, Sortie' at the Liège fans as they left in ever increasing numbers after each goal. He got his French/Belgian patois from the signs above the exit doors. They seemed to understand. We eventually won 7–0 and we were so drunk that we thought at one stage we had seen Eddie McGoldrick score an individual wonder goal.

How pissed were we? My only other recollection of that night was singing 'Happy Birthday' to Ian Wright even though he wasn't even playing … I don't think. We eventually had about two hours kip in the hotel that we had craved for not long before and then headed back to the bar for a farewell drink to thank them for looking after us (plying us with drink and not barring us). Unfortunately we developed a flat tyre so we were able to stay a touch longer. I thought my chance for darts revenge may come up but apparently Bertrand Bristow had seriously overdone it the night before with his celebrations and wouldn't be coming out to play anytime soon. An uneventful journey home probably due to the fact we didn't play our Kent village name game.

Arsenal shareholder Darren Epstein was also there. He told me,

Liège away felt like the whole of Highbury went to Belgium. Literally everyone I knew went to that game. To this day I'm not sure if we were great or that Liège were truly woeful. It was the game McGoldrick scored that great goal. He'll forever remembered for that … only because he was one of the all-time worst signings for the club.

I remember going to the restaurant across the ground and ordering Burger American and it arriving as a raw burger mixed with egg. I ended up arguing with the waiter in semi-French about how ridiculous it was that anyone would ever order something like that!

I'm not sure why, but after the game there was trouble between the Liège fans, so it was a bit dicey getting out of the ground.

The former BBC sports producer Steve Tongue, football correspondent for *The Independent on Sunday*, who covered the game and was a member of the press there that night told me,

With Standard Liège, who'd beaten Cardiff very easily, you'd think there was a bit of quality there. However apart from that 3-0 home defeat by Coventry on the opening day the second-leg turned into just about the most untypical Arsenal performance of the season. Being 3–0 up from the first game you'd have thought George would just want to keep it tight, maybe nick one more goal to avoid any hint of problems … but to win 7–0 away from home without Ian Wright. We were all in shock on the flight home!

Winning by such a margin away from home is impressive but to do so without your main striker (Ian Wright was rested on the night as he picked up what would be a costly yellow in the first leg) was doubly so.

Daily Mirror's headline was, 'Seven Gunner Salute' while *The Times* went with, 'Inspired Arsenal Complete the Route of Liège'. The Arsenal scorers read like a litany of joy: Alan Smith, 3 minutes, Ian Selley 21, Tony Adams 37, Kevin Campbell 41 and 79, Paul Merson 71, and the unlikely Eddie McGoldrick on 81 minutes. The result ensured Arsenal were now unbeaten in twenty-three cup ties dating back nearly two years.

A nonplussed George Graham said at the time,

It was a breath-taking performance, especially by the three lads up front. Every time we went forward it looked like we would score, but I would have to say the opposition's defending was very poor.

It was probably our best performance in my time at the club and I just wish we could reproduce this quality more often. But it was a great night for Arsenal and the players deserve a really big pat on the back.

It was instructive that Liège's Arie Haan declined to talk to the press afterwards. Perhaps he was too busy watching videos of English football…

The brilliant Amy Lawrence recalled,

I missed Standard Liège away because I was on crutches. […] I distinctly remember going to Highbury on crutches to watch a screening of the away game in Belgium – or it may have been a pub in Highbury I can't recall exactly because my memory is so bad these days! But I definitely watched the game in N5 on crutches.

It was a classic moment of disbelief when Eddie McGoldrick hit number seven and even before that when the last few goals went in. It was a good performance which was important for the status of Arsenal in Europe that season. To achieve such an eye-opening win made people sit up and think 'wow. That was a good result by Arsenal'.

European competition at the time was so unnatural and bizarre for Arsenal, it did feel they had to make a name for themselves and the 7–0 in Belgium helped do that. It was almost like Arsenal had a slight inferiority complex about being in Europe at that time. Certainly compared to clubs like Liverpool and Manchester United, as well as teams like Aston Villa and Nottingham Forest and so on who'd won European Cups around the time.

The fact the only European success the club had was in 1970 meant Arsenal's European record didn't tally with Arsenal's domestic record at that time. Arsenal weren't held in high esteem or high up the record books in Europe compared to other clubs. The club's European CV wasn't strong. So to go away and win 7–0 to a perfectly established team with a European pedigree of sorts was quite meaningful after all they weren't going away to Malta or Cyprus or Lithuania and putting seven past them for example.

What I remember from that trip as a fresh-faced twenty-one year old on my first European away was everything seemed to be one long adventure so different to anything I'd encountered from domestic away games.

I recall being in an all-night bar in Brussels, with the owner happy to stay open as long as we bought beers, however he drew the line at us singing Arsenal songs and instead insisted we could sing 'nice songs, like the Beatles'. So every time we felt like singing, which as the night wore on admittedly became more frequent, we'd sing Beatles songs instead. I once spent six hours in a karaoke bar in Tokyo during the 2002 World Cup, and the experience in Brussels seemed like a precursor but without actually having a karaoke machine. Or even a jukebox for that matter. At the end of the night, or should I say at daybreak, the poor man was at his wits end and said pleadingly, 'I've had enough of the Beatles now'. I still wonder whether he's listened to them since bearing in mind how badly out of tune we were and how strong the Belgian beer was.

We then slept under the Atomium in the car before curiosity got the better of our young selves and we made the nearby trip to the derelict Heysel Stadium. It had been boarded up and long shut, years before its re-emergence as one of the Belgian venues in 2000. It felt eerie thinking what happened there as we walked around the grey crumbling concrete walls.

It was to be another twelve years before a £140,000 sculpture was unveiled at the new Heysel stadium, to commemorate the disaster. The humble monument, a sundial designed by French artist Patrick Rimoux, included Italian and Belgian stone with the poem 'Funeral Blues' by W. H. Auden symbolising the three counties involved in the tragedy. Thirty-nine lights also shine, one for each person who died that fateful night.

However, there was none of that in November 1993. Just a horrific reminder of the deaths with a large, awful piece of graffiti that read, '–39'. I wondered then, as I still wonder now, why no-one bothered to whitewash the writing as it was poor a taste piece of graffiti as I have ever seen.

The night before the game we stayed in Charleroi. The name was to become synonymous with England and Germany, who played out a low grade 1–0 win in favour of the Three Lions at Euro 2000, along with a considerable number of plastic furniture hurled through the air by fans on the day coupled with high powered water cannon being employed.

That night in Liège, because the authorities were wary of a repeat of the trouble marring the previous round when more than 100 Cardiff City fans were detained before and after playing Liège, we were allocated our very own police escort that night. When I say police escort I mean a tired old local policeman and his even more straggly Alsatian. We then experienced the unusual concept of being followed from bar to bar by our own personal police force of this unlikely pairing as they waited to see what trouble we would get up to. When they realised we were far more harm to ourselves in drunken accidents than any threat to the locals and their bars, and after declining a beer from us for the umpteenth time (including offering a bowl of dark Belgian beer to his utterly bored Alsatian), they left us alone.

Whereupon we proceeded to get incredibly drunk on strong Belgian beer including many shades of different fruit beers. As we said of that night a long time afterwards we were years ahead of our time drinking colourful but potent alcohol, long before red and blue alcopops had ever been invented.

The next morning we headed to the ground and despite all the warnings from various English sources we simply bought three tickets for the home-end. All we were requested to show was our passports for them to photocopy and for a studious bespectacled man to take a photo of us. When I say passports I actually mean that folded, beige piece of card that passed for a British Visitor's Passport. How times have changed.

I like to think that somewhere in the bowels of Standard Liège's new stadium, also rebuilt for Euro 2000, there's a room full of papers and official looking documents they didn't throw out as they weren't sure what they were. And among them I like to think there are photocopies of three young lads looking extremely hungover complete with a crappy old A4 piece of paper showing our visitors' passports.

The rest of the day flew by in a blur of more strong Belgian beer as we bumped into groups of other young wide-eyed Gooners on their first trip abroad following The Arsenal and shared stories of strange occurrences. I also recall hearing a bar we'd been drinking in just had been smashed up minutes after we had staggered out of it heading for a bar nearer the ground apparently by Liège fans looking to nail travelling Gooners.

At the ground, which to me didn't seem as good a standard as a second or third tier English ground let alone one that played host to regular European football, I saw water cannon trucks for the first time aimed at football fans. Although we had tickets for the home end we simply walked to the dilapidated away end and got in. It was then we saw hordes of young lads drinking lager from plastic cups becoming increasingly – or so we thought – drunk. Overjoyed we immediately went to the bar where Matt asked the barman in perfect French 'is this beer alcoholic?' Before being met with a wide but incredulous smile, a shrug of the shoulders and the line, 'No of course not!'

The game itself was unbelievable. Even though 'One-Nil-To-The-Arsenal' had yet to be sung the team, and us supporters, were all too aware of our battling defensive spirit along with our ever-decreasing strike rate. Similar to many who were there that night in Liège as the goals rained in any fear or worry about 3-0 not being enough quickly dissipated into a feeling of pure joy – then surprise, then disbelief and then absurdity. The only other match I can liken such a complete change of emotions to is when I was at the Olympia Stadion Munich watching England beat Germany 5-1 one glorious evening in September 2001.

I also recall there being a makeshift band at the stand to our right at the Scllessin. The band looked like they'd enjoyed themselves that afternoon also, as they parped and trumpeted various pieces that sounded what they were – drunk blokes trying to play musical instruments but were too hammered to make it sound harmonious. As the goals flew in they were joined by a ludicrous figure in a woolly bobble hat who proceeded to dance the Funky Chicken up and down the ever-emptying row, oblivious to the fact his team were becoming a laughing stock. It certainly made the fans who took in a bedsheet with the message, 'Spurs Supporters Liège Branch' look ridiculous. They had brazenly hung it over the seats higher up to our right. How we laughed as it became 5- and 6-0. The fact Eddie McGoldrick scored the seventh (his only Arsenal goal) simply made the night more surreal as many chanted, 'Tottenham/Tottenham: What's the score?'

Stunned but delighted, at the final whistle all we could do was clap, as the pure emotion and sheer surprise at the result meant we were far too drained to do anything else. Unfortunately outside we were somehow herded onto a train by Belgian Robocops which we found out was going to take/send/deport four carriages of Gooners to Ostend. It wasn't a thought which appealed, not least because our car was in the centre of Liège. There'd been a bit of trouble during the day caused by the home fans, not Arsenal, and a few people on the now increasingly tense train were sporting cuts and bruises.

A lad next to us said loudly to a policeman, 'I've been legged half-way around your fucking town, been fired at with water cannon, been herded onto a train that's going to Ostend for you to deport us for no reason and my bloody car's parked in the centre of Liège.' The riot policeman eyed him contemptuously before replying coldly, 'Yes. But has anyone got any serious problems'. It was then many in our carriage decided to make a sharp exit. The train being of old stock with doors opening manually was ideally constructed for people to jump out before it pulled off. So there we were running through train tracks and away from a train we had no wish to be on.

I always find when you run when you're very drunk your legs somehow overtake the rest of your body so it always feels like you're just about to topple over. Thankfully we never did, although I shudder to think what would have happened if there had been other moving trains in that goods yard. Eventually we found ourselves on a bus the police had commandeered from somewhere. I'm not sure even they knew what to do with us all by now, so they simply rounded up Arsenal fans who'd 'escaped' from the Ostend-bound train, put them in four or five buses and took us back to the city centre. As we were far too drunk to even contemplate driving we did what any self-respecting English travelling fan would do, and found a late night dive, staying there drinking till dawn. As we staggered back to the car which was only around the corner we found we need to urinate. As the car was parked near the city centre, but in a less-than-salubrious place we relieved ourselves in a large empty bottle of cola we had in the car. For some reason we then left it on our roof. A few hours later we were woken by drunk vagrants shouting in the street next to our car. It was only then we realised they'd appropriated our bottle of liquid we'd left on the roof, and were merrily glugging from the bottle. Those unfortunate vagrants and their unexpected action pretty much summed up that trip, and the result ... as you could say it was piss-taking at its finest.

5

Torino vs Arsenal: In the Witch's Garden

European Cup Winners' Cup, quarter-final, first leg. 2 March 1994. Torino 0 Arsenal 0.

> Some are created for beauty and some for use; and there are some which one can do without altogether.
>
> Hans Christian Andersen, *There Is a Difference*.

> *Un Partita Brutto* (An Ugly Game)
>
> *Gazetta della Sport*

> The best policed hangover in the world.
>
> Arsenal fan Matthew Bleasby in the Stadio delle Alpi.

Alan Smith is feeling more comfortable with my friend Dan and I, realising we're lifelong Arsenal fans, with a genuine love of the club he graced for so long, in such a dignified, impressive manner. He stirs his coffee and leans forward slightly almost imperceptibly which to me signals a willingness to engage. His body language is now less tense, friendlier, and his face reveals a hint of passion. Maybe he is enjoying recalling that cup run too. Maybe not all interviews with have to be a guarded battle.

Alan Smith says to us, his eyes lost in recall but his memory as sharp as his finishing ever was,

> There were a lot of difficult challenges and difficult teams we played in the cup run of 1993/94 and the year after. Defenders would mark you differently, there'd be more man-on-man, they'd mark you that little bit tighter. There'd be different tricks you'd face in Europe compared to domestically.
>
> I remember Silenzi having a nailed on chance at the Stadio delle Alpi and missing it. And you suddenly think for a second, 'Hold on, it might be our year'.

At the revelation that sportsmen are human too, that not everyone takes one game at is comes no matter how much they try to and how much they insist to us mere mortals they try to, I follow-up with a question seizing on that endearing admission. I ask, 'When did you start thinking the 1994 team had a chance to win the European Cup Winners Cup trophy?' Alan thinks hard. Almost too hard before responding with,

> I don't think we ever thought that throughout the entire run. I don't think we ever thought it was going to be our trophy. You get to the final and you think you might have a chance but that Torino game was a grind. The 0–0 in Italy was a grind. It was a shocking game. Torino in the quarters – they were a tough nut to crack …

And again the memories come flooding back. Arsenal Football Club was the first English representative to play in Turin since the terrible disaster at Heysel in May 1985. Eight long years had passed. Thirty-nine people had died at Heysel. Thirty-nine people went to watch a football match and never came home. Fifty-six died at the Bradford Fire. The same day, 11 May 1985, a teenager died when a wall gave way at St Andrews after rioting between Birmingham City and Leeds United. On 15 April 1989 ninety-six football fans tragically lost their lives at Hillsborough.

The 1980s were a tough time to be an English football fan. Yet from those lowest lows a new spirit rose in the game. A new beginning formed with the realisation that things couldn't go on the way they were in terms of hooliganism but also in terms of treating all football fans the way Margaret Thatcher did, as potential criminals.

The years 1985 to 1991 were a barren time punctuated with periods of true pain and loss, interspersed with shock. For how else can you describe a loved one dying at a football match? There was also denial by many clubs, administrators and officials that there was actually anything wrong with English football. Others took just as radical viewpoint in that everything was wrong with English football, with only an identity card proposed as an answer. A card that would have, for all intents and purposes, killed English football stone dead at the time. Even if it's ironic that most clubs and most supporters, certainly in the top divisions today, use some sort of membership card as an indicator of support, at a price of course.

There was also a prolonged period of self-loathing, when English football fans genuflected at the riches of continental talent which could soar far higher than our domestic gods. For example Arrigo Sacchi's imperious Milan teams of the late 1980s before there was resignation at the situation. Until a new found pride emerged at the heroic performances of the Three Lions at Italia 1990. Therefore when English clubs were admitted back into Europe in September 1990, before Arsenal joined in 1991 as champions of the vintage Alan Smith mentioned, it was still to be a further three years before any English team played in Turin. And that team was to be Arsenal – with her 3,000 loyal travelling fans entering the bear pit of the Stadio delle Alpi – or Witches Garden as Hans Christian Andersen phrased one of his immortal fairy-tales.

One Night in Turin, on 2 March 1994, another fairytale just as improbable as the ones Odenses' favourite son penned was starting to take shape. I ask Stewart Houston if he recalls the match at the Stadio delle Alpi, Torino's unloved home. There's a brief silence between us so I tell him, as much in conversation as way of a prompt, 'I was in Torino as a fan. I remember Silenzi missing an open goal when it was easier for him to score. It may well have been a crucial miss in the context of the tie. When did you think, if at all, we might have a chance in this tournament?'

Stewart thinks deeply and in his deep accent replies bullishly,

We'd a chance there too where we could've scored but didn't so it wasn't just them who had possibilities to score. However it's true you do get instances like that which are turning points in games, key moments that turn games. But yes, when someone's missed an open goal you do think 'well that's a get out of jail card'. But that's football. Somebody should score but doesn't and it changes the whole game or tie. But what I found playing against Torino, and Parma that year and Sampdoria the year after, was all Italian players are tactically well-drilled and astute. Which was a real challenge for us as a team. But I have to say a challenge which we relished and one which we proved to have the upper hand in – to the surprise of many.

People say Serie A was arguably the world's strongest league in the 1990s, certainly one of the strongest if not the strongest. Of course it's still strong now but back then it was far above say the Spanish and German league which may not be the case today. They were a top football nation then, a very well-respected football nation with the Milan's and Juve's of course.

They were always very well-conditioned with a very good technique and technical ability which allied with their tactical nous made them very hard to beat. Which was why it so was important to take them back to Highbury at the very level with the scores level and if we couldn't get the away goal then it was crucial not to concede over there, and we didn't.

As I mentioned Layth, we did spent a lot of time on the opposition, studying their strengths and weaknesses, but we also spent quite a number of training sessions trying to counter the tactical ability of the Italians. It was hard work, and there were a few groans, but everyone in that team and squad bought into it which ultimately made the hard work pay off.

I am impressed by talk of hard work. I don't want my teams or my managers not to focus on the opposition. It worries me even if we believe we are the better side. I have always felt reassured when you hear players or managers and assistant managers tell the world they've studied the opposition and put in the hours on tactics designed to outfox our opponents either in an attacking sense or a defensive sense. And for a tie like Torino the defensive work was crucial to Arsenal's chances of further progress.

I ask Stewart 'how important was Tony Adams to the team during that tie? Everyone knows he scored the winner at home to Torino in the tense second-leg at Highbury. But he was immense defensively, as a leader and a centre-half in the heat of the battle in Italy.'

Stewart replies immediately with relish indicating the respect he and George Graham had for Tony Adams by saying,

Tony loved a physical battle, absolutely loved it. But don't forget the Italians had that physical presence as well which played right into Tony's hands. The game's changed as you well know Layth but back then there was always a 'testing' period in those European games in which both sides would test each other out to find out how strong they were and sometimes we'd force ourselves onto the opposition. The players had no problem with that. The Italians could give it out too. Teams would test Tony physically too. Which he loved.

Make no mistake some of that Torino team could look after themselves just as much as Tony and some of our players could. We found, and certainly Tony Adams found, the physical challenge of a battle more a 'charge'. A buzz, something which electrified him into giving an even better performance. He rose to the challenge of Torino, both home and away, as did everyone in that Arsenal team.

I mention tactics to Stewart again. I tentatively suggest that George and he laid the template for midfielders screening the back four, which is so commonplace in today's football. A screening which effectively turned a back four into a back six when under pressure, so I ask him, 'How important was that system Arsenal appeared to employ during the latter stages of that run against Torino, PSG, and Parma. The fact that defensively minded midfielders such as Ian Selley, John Jensen and Stephen Morrow, for the final if not Torino away, could drop back to solidify a back four when required?'

The thoughtful Houston warming to the task of talking tactics answers with a studiously fascinating reply,

We found when we did our homework on sides in Europe, and certainly towards the business end of the competition, that most sides played with 'three' in midfield. Which also meant if you were playing a team in which defenders looked to push forward we could be left with a situation where you get completely outgunned in the middle of the park. Which is dangerous. We felt it was imperative to address that situation in the 'engine room' which, as you rightly said, was the main reason we went along those lines defensively. We wanted cover in midfield as that was where we felt the real battle field was but our system also allowed players to drop back to cover defensively. Not all the time of course because you can get overloaded in midfield, which then means your back line has got much more work to do. But we'd change the tactical formation from 4-4-2 to what was 4-3-3 because if you want to win games generally 'winning' the midfield is the best place to start. If you play 4-4-2 in those type of games you effectively only have two men in the middle of the park and may perhaps cede space and possession. Whereas with 4-3-3 you have the extra man to help win the battle. Which also helps to push back their defenders who may have been pushing forward previously, which has the added bonus of helping to take on their midfielders too, changing the whole momentum and impetus of the opposition and making yourselves not only harder to beat but also more of a threat offensively too.

It was an instructive conversation on tactics as it was made simple by Houston. No wonder the players bought into such revolutionary and innovative tactics when it was explained to them the way he explained it to me. It made such sense. And it worked in against Torino a more defensive character to the team, which would result in one of the dreariest 0-0s I can ever recall. But as someone who was there I didn't care so long as we didn't lose. And nor did Arsenal's team and management.

I talk to Patrick Barclay about Torino. Barclay, as everyone knows, is a keen student of the game and is one of the most knowledgeable football journalists there is. I ask him if it was Liam Brady who introduced him to Italian food when he interviewed him at Juventus in the early 1980s.

It's true! I knew a bit about pasta and already had a bolognese recipe which I used at home but Liam showed me a restaurant in Turin called Due Lampione where I learned the joys of grilled zucchini and egg-plant and osso buco and the rest. Later, after he moved from Juventus to Inter, he and his wife Sarah kindly invited me to stay a night at their house on the banks of Lake Como. It was an extremely pleasant house. But there was a vast and ornate place on the other side of the lake and, when I mentioned it, Liam didn't look all that pleased that I was so impressed. I found out later that it was Karl-Heinz Rummenigge's mansion. Maybe Rummenigge was on bigger wages than Liam!

I've always liked Liam. For a truly outstanding player (which you had to be to star in Serie A in his time) he never had any 'side' to him. And he enjoyed the company of some journalists, none more than the late, lamented Reg Drury.

Lapping up these snippets about Brady I then ask him about Torino as a club and immediately his voice rises again which to me indicates his passion about a particular topic.

I remember writing a piece about Torino because I was fascinated by the history of Torino. This was because they were the Italian equivalent of the Busby Babes who perished because after the Second World War the plane that was carrying them crashed at Superga in Turin killing them all.

That team had been described as 'the best Italian team ever' and, at the time, they would arguably have been the best team in Europe. Although of course there was no measure back then. I was fascinated by Torino's history so please take whatever you like from my *Observer* pieces on that run by all means help yourself Layth.

I've been to Turin many times to report on football matches. When I first went to Turin it was the Stadio Communale in the 70s and 80s but when the Stadio delle Alpi was built it was a terrible, soulless place. It was a bit like Stoke City, it seemed to be cold all the time, despite what the weather was like outside! The place sticks in my memory as being one of cold concrete even though there were some great games there, in 1990 for example I covered the England match against Germany in the World Cup semi-final. I think even the Stadio delle Alpi rocked during that game. I think it was famous for never being full from the day of construction to the day of demolition, it just always seemed to be one of those jinxed stadiums.

Of course it was nowhere near full for the goalless draw Arsenal game in March 1994.

I mention to Patrick that I went to the game which, apart from a pair of dreadful 0-0s against Birmingham City, was the worst 0–0 I'd ever seen. Patrick smiled wryly and replied simply, 'Yes it was a rather tedious game wasn't it?'

An old friend of mine Matthew Bleasby, who had accompanied Guy Wiseman and myself to the already legendary Liège trip again came with us again to Europe to watch Arsenal, this time in Turin.

His recollection of Torino away was of booking through a tour operator called UF tours.

They'd based us in Milan, because we were the first English team to play in Turin since Heysel and it was deemed safer to stay in a hotel on the outskirts of another Italian city and head over to Turin by coach on the day of the game. So we woke up on match-day a little shabby after drinking the previous day in Milan which for some reason had seen us stumble into a thoroughfare which had a number of 'ladies of the night' shall we say. But what was more surprising to us innocent travellers was the realisation they were actually transvestites. Again I have to say our insight into their sexual orientation was because one of them, dressing in a fetching mini-skirt and elegantly holding an umbrella, asked us for a cigarette –in a really deep voice. One of our friends was actually taking a photo of us at the time and captured the look on our faces at the moment of realisation. I think the line someone said just after summed it up best when they exclaimed, 'that woman's a bloke!'

On the day of the game someone had correctly anticipated the ground would be dry and that they would be unlikely to let us have a look around Turin pre-match to have a few liveners. So in order to ensure that the day passed with at least a couple of drinks we decided to smuggle a bottle of tequila on board our Turin bound coach. It certainly made for an eventful coach trip. Clearly the significance of us being the first

English team to play in Turin since Heysel had not been lost on the Caribineri who went to ridiculous extents to keep the Arsenal fans away from the locals.

Our coaches were met by police outside of Turin and escorted in by what seemed to be an unnecessarily large police operation. At the ground we were ushered in quickly though they had time to relieve us of any loose change, coins and lighters. In the ground they had ensured there were blocks of empty seats either side and in front so that the pitch could have only been reached by an Olympic javelin gold medallist even if you had smuggled something in. I had hid my lighter in my sock although I had no intention of using it for anything other than to chain smoke my way through the duty-frees in a bid to thwart the inevitable hangover.

The over-the-top segregation and policing was a little surreal considering the ground was half-empty. The post-Italia 1990 Channel Four Serie A love-in had shown us Ultras putting on match day pyrotechnics and giant flag waving shows. But the Torino Ultra clearly didn't feel that the visit of Arsenal was worthy of such a show and those that did turn up barely rarely raised a voice. To be fair it was turgid stuff on display and little for either side to get excited about. Even if they set off flares and firecrackers which covered the ground in smoke just after kick-off. It was very much life imitating art, as the tactical defensive masterpiece planned by George Graham progressed on the pitch, it mirrored the hangover off it.

In the context of the tie 0–0 was a good result, which a Tony Adams header in the second-leg would undermine the importance of. I'm pretty sure we celebrated it with a few drinks later that night in Milan, but my overriding memory of Turin is the best policed hangover in the world.

The Gooner editor Kevin Whitcher adds,

The quarter-final saw Arsenal draw against the Italian side Torino. This was in the days when only the actual champions took part in what was then the nascent Champions League so the line-ups in both of the other European competitions were relatively strong. The other six quarter-finalists were Real Madrid, Paris St Germain, Benfica, Ajax, Parma and Bayer Leverkusen. All potential winners of the trophy.

I made the journey to the first-leg in Italy on a coach that left Euston two days before the game in the company of Warren who had been on the Liège trip too. The trip was run by a Manchester concern called UA Tours. It was memorable for a few things. Although there were two drivers on the trip one was evidently falling asleep at the wheel in the early hours of the night as we could see the coach weaving around a bit, although fortunately he woke up a bit after someone had a word. There was on-board TV and I can recall someone had brought along a load of Simpsons videos which are all I can remember watching. One guy got a very bloody nose due to falling drunk down the stairs and was told he could have the trip free to avoid any compensation issues against UA Tours.

Entering the north of Italy, which was white with snow, was a fantastic experience. The night before the game and the following one we were billeted up in an out of town hotel somewhere near Milan. The coach driver couldn't find it so had to hire a taxi to lead him there. The hotel was pretty much the middle of nowhere, although at least there was a bar that served beer within walking distance.

On the day of the game, we took the coach to Turin. Police presence was heavy. We were dropped outside the ground and UA Tours had included match tickets in the home sections as part of the package but told us to use them for the away entrance as that was what the police wanted. Knowing the likely confinement after the game, Warren and I slipped the cordon (not wearing colours helped) and took a stroll before entering in our allocated entrance without an eyebrow being raised. We even got into discussion with some Torino fans during the game and they were fine with us being there given our lack of demonstrative behaviour (which was probably what gave us away in Italy!). Still there was hardly anything to get demonstrative about. Arsenal killed the game in a David Hillier denial masterclass and it was probably one of the dullest matches the Stadio delle Alpi ever witnessed.

However, 0–0 was a decent enough result, which Arsenal capitalized on in a tight return-leg, with only a Tony Adams goal separating the sides. Urban myth has it that Osama Bin Laden attended this match having spent time at the Finsbury Park Mosque around this period although, frankly, I suspect it didn't really happen.

Mike Francis explained,

We took around 4,500 fans to Turin for the goalless quarter-final and a similar quantity of flags judging by the impressive display in the Stadio delle Alpi, including one huge one at the front emblazoned with the words 'Arsenal's Beano in Torino'.

This was one of the earliest excursions organised by Miles from the Alexandra Pub who would go on to form Sport Options which has been flying fans to sports events all over the world. One of the reasons for the success of his trips was that they ensured the fans were allowed some time in the destination and would generally organise a local restaurant for lunch and some liquid refreshment which always goes down well!

As for the game itself the *Guardian's* headline was a trifle harsh it completely missed the point of how disciplined our tactics were when it blasted 'Arsenal Revel in the Goalless and the Guileless'. While the reporter David Lacey, never one to dance on the club's grave when a strained analogy would do, joyfully, proclaimed, '"Arsenal's Beano in Torino" said one banner – well, it was if one liked cold vermicelli washed down with warm Frascati', adding 'the match was boring in the extreme. By comparison the Maastrict debate seemed like Hancock's Half Hour.'

I much prefer this match report, taken from the *Gazetta della Sport* the morning after the night before, which pretty much summed it up:

Date-line Turin: Nothing had happened after the first ninety minutes so Turin and Arsenal will compete in the race for the Cup Winners' Cup semi-final at Highbury in two weeks' time. It was a very tactical match in which Turin, conscious of their own limits, fought above all to not take chances. They certainly did not fight too hard to create authentic dangers for Seaman who remained, pretty much, inactive.

With Mondonico's team appearing to lack their traditional capacity to fight back in adversity to keep them angry, sharp, very dangerous. However Silenzi's black day – the solitude of Francescoli, the concern of Jarni and Fortunato – saw to it that Torino did not threaten Arsenal.

Arsenal tried to win, at least at the start, but not even Graham was willing to take a risk.

And that is why it ended in a predictable 0–0 draw. For the first period the travellers from London played practically in their own half. The English, according to tradition, usually play without holding back but not last night. The defence kept their shape with full-backs Dixon and Winterburn along the flanks opposite a clumsy Jarni and a strangely checked Mussi. The centre-halves, Adams and the giant Bould, closed every gap Francescoli had without effort and, producing an unhappy Silenzi in the process, were almost stationed at the 22nd metre. And the mobile defensive midfielder Hillier gave a hand to his colleagues playing in the centre positions with absolute fluency.

In the control room of central midfield the aggressive Davis forced Fortunato into a more withdrawn position, while the committed Dane Jensen took on Venturin in bitter duels, as the imaginative Merson tried to provide a delicious final ball for Campbell and Smith and the jewel Wright. The attacking three, by luck, were brilliant at guarding the great Sottil in a superb way but at the same time their attacking instincts were rendered incapable by the relentless Gregucci to the point that captain Fusi didn't have to do much.

It was a monotonous game however because Jarni and Mussi closed with effectiveness cutting off any possibility for England to exploit one of their most traditional and dreaded weapons crossing from the by-line. So in the short spaces the Gunners didn't shine. Merson's feet were not able to communicate with his team mates' and when Campbell and Davies tried it they didn't ever succeed in getting the timing right to allow the possibility of infiltrating Turin's lines properly.

Turin were left increasingly desperate as they threw long passes from Venturin or Fortunato forward but Silenzi wasn't having a great evening. He couldn't shine and Francescoli, who had the right style, was often left alone faced with three opponents. It was logical then that the two squads were remarried with the misery of a goalless draw.

After the interval the music didn't change. The race maintained its connotations. Exasperatedly tactical with a Turin side trying to avoid conceding any goals at home but at the same time were not very convincing with its own offensive strategy. However, Turin did stage the occasional attack with Fortunato who headed the ball over the bar after a cross from Jarni. Arsenal continued in its own sickly possession of the ball without ever pushing forward with the necessary conviction, which was also thanks to Turin's impeccable defence.

So, the second-half finished even more deprived of emotion than the first-half. Mondonico prepared the entrance of Carbone to liven up their manoeuvres but he had to first replace Sottil, a victim of cramp, with Sinigaglia. So he took over the now tamed Campbell and Mossi clung onto Merson. Carbone finally entered to applause replacing Silenzi. He became the protagonist in an instant that sowed the panic in the English defence and gave enthusiasm to the *tifosi* in the *curva*, but nothing concrete came of his efforts.

So to London they must travel to settle the tie after *una partita brutto*.

'The Goals Are All Closed', *Gazetta della Sport*, 3 March 1994.

Two supporters of the Italian club Torino were charged yesterday with possessing explosives at their team's European Cup Winners' Cup quarter-final first-leg. Salvatore Barno and Luca Perino, both aged twenty-eight, were alleged to have had eight small cylinders packed with a mixture of weed-killer, sugar and potassium chloride at the Della Alpi stadium on 2 March.

Barno was arrested as he went to collect the cylinders fifteen minutes before the end of the game. An Italian news agency said the devices would have had the effect of small bombs if they had been used against Arsenal fans.

'Torino Fans Charged', *Guardian*, 20 March 1994.

6

Arsenal vs Torino: The Steadfast Tin Soldier

European Cup Winners' Cup, quarter-final, second-leg. 15 March 1994. Arsenal 1 Torino 0. (Arsenal won 1-0 on aggregate).

> Brave soldier, never fear.
>
> Hans Christian Andersen, *The Steadfast Tin Soldier*.

> George always made sure the players put the work in during the week because he believed your performance on a Saturday or Wednesday stemmed from the hard work you put in during training.
>
> Stewart Houston.

> The relief at the final whistle was something else. Strangers in the East Stand leaving and shaking hands, hugging each other. Arsenal v Torino under the floodlights at Highbury was an incredible night.
>
> Jem Maidment.

Arsenal had endured a somewhat disappointing and inconsistent winter in the five month gap between the Liège and Torino ties. Results were patchy from November to March. Guy and I were at a great 4-0 win at Swindon on Boxing Day but I also remember Bolton winning in the FA Cup at Highbury.

I ask Stewart Houston if the patchy results over the winter period solidified their growing belief that Arsenal could achieve something in Europe. His reply is instructive as it highlights not only the expectation levels at a club like Arsenal but also the fact that football is very much a squad game now, something it certainly wasn't in 1993/94, which to a club like Arsenal may have had negative effects not readily acknowledged at the time.

He tells me emphatically,

> If we go back one step, the reason we were finding it difficult in the league was because of those European games. They were gruelling and we only had a small

squad. There was no sense of 'rotation' as there is now. For the most part our players would play in Europe, travel back in the early hours and then play on the Saturday. For example I remember the year after we played an absolutely intense semi-final against Sampdoria in Genoa on the Thursday with extra time and penalties and then had to play a league game at QPR at 3.00 p.m. on the Saturday.

So going back to 1993/94 we changed the team around a bit after the ties with Odense and Liège, after all of them in fact, but there was not the rotation you get these days when you might get four, five or even six players who would be rested from a league game following a European away, […] we didn't have the players. So people can say our league form was patchy but that was the reason. Of course the travelling didn't help. We'd be home at three, four or five in the morning with players who'd be playing intense league games a matter of days later. Of course it still happens now but my point is you have far bigger squads to deal with it. Your body becomes 'distorted' and it takes you a couple of days to reboot itself.

Another point, don't forget, is we played full-strength sides in the League Cup and FA Cup and the League Cup had replays and two-legged second rounds in those days. You can even say there was a bigger spotlight on us because we were in Europe and competing on a prestigious stage may have tied us a little psychologically. So all those factors had repercussions which perhaps weren't taken into account at the time, or even when looking back.

We also had intense training sessions too. George always made sure the players put the work in during the week because he believed your performance on a Saturday, or Wednesday, stemmed from the hard work you put in during training. He demanded high standards from everyone during the week and he refused to let standards slip at any time. It was ingrained in the ethos at the time. At times I may have thought it was a little over the top but it was ingrained in us and it worked because we won the European Cup Winners' Cup.

The players may have had a few moans and groans about it but it worked so they just got on and did it. It was never overly long though. It was never two or three hour sessions or anything like that. It was short sharp and intense.

It was an impassioned explanation of the mental and physical demands placed on Arsenal players that season. Demands that may not have been readily admitted or even understood by players and fans alike. Which makes the achievements of that season even more admirable.

I ask Stewart about the respect players had for George and himself at the time:

There's no 'I' in team. We had to be a team. Anyone who's ever played in any sort of team at any sort of level knows that. So if you didn't want to be part of a team, well, you could move on … and we'd help make arrangements for you to move on. It was all about the team.

We tried to be as clear as possible in what we expected from the players and if there were any issues we'd try to address it and make sure they understood and to their huge credit they all responded. Of course winning football matches breeds confidence. It's as simple as that. Winning football matches leads to wining trophies and trips to Europe to win more trophies.

George was a hard taskmaster, it's been well documented over the years, but he expected a certain work ethic from all the players and he got it because the players just got on with it.

And my word did our Arsenal heroes just get on with it. Amy Lawrence recalled,

Serie A was the glamour league in the early 1990s and I think it was right that the English league had a little bit of an inferiority complex in general about football in Italy. The biggest money was in Italy and the best players were in Italy. It was an exotic league full of fascination. This was the very beginning of the Premier League when it was still in its second season, when the glamour, the coverage and the money hadn't got going properly yet.

So the changes coming into force in English football still hadn't taken hold yet and we were just at a really very nascent time whereas Italy was the establishment and Serie A representatives were a little daunting. It's so long ago I can't recall too much about the day unfortunately but I do remember the second-leg at Highbury.

Nearly all of those games that season I was there as a fan rather than reporting on them. It's worth remembering 'One-Nil-To-The-Arsenal' hadn't actually been born at the time of that game against Torino in the quarter-finals at Highbury. It came of course in the away-end at Paris at half-time in the semi-final. The 1–0 win against Torino, in many ways, was the *hors d'oeuvre* if you like as the momentum that would turn into 'One-Nil-To-The-Arsenal' was born that night. The evidence was right there that tense evening at Highbury.

The experienced Fleet Street journalist and BBC sports producer Steve Tongue recalled the tie telling me,

By the quarter-final there seemed to be eight decent teams left and I think George Graham was a bit wary of Torino, perhaps because he thought as a classic Italian team their strengths might be the same as Arsenal's. So I'm sure he was pleased with the 0–0 over there and even more so with a set-piece goal to win the home-leg. I was surprised little Carbone didn't play a bigger part over the two games. He was a clever player who seemed to change clubs every year in Italy and finally settled down when he came to England with Sheffield Wednesday a couple of years later. So their main striker was Andrea Silenzi who always seemed more of British striker than an Italian one but was, of course, an utter flop when Nottingham Forest signed him.

Author of five Arsenal books including *All Guns Blazing, Rebels for the Cause, Top Guns, Highbury* and his latest best-seller *Red Letter Days*, Jon Spurling told me,

I view George Graham's teams with as much pride and affection as any of Arsene Wenger's sides. I'm an extremely pragmatic Arsenal fan. Being fourty-five means I've seen Arsenal win ugly and I've also seen them win beautiful. For me there's always more than one way to win a football match and I think anyone who thinks differently is deluding themselves. The Arsenal team of 1994 were the ultimate 'bus-parkers' of their era.

It was before the term had even been invented. It wasn't a vintage Arsenal team not even by the standards of George's blue-collar sides. It functioned due to a watertight defence, a limpet-like midfield and Ian Wright. Some of the football they played was awful and totally forgettable. But the Cup Winners Cup run will always stick in my memory. I went to the Highbury games against Torino and PSG. I loved the sense of occasion because I'd never seen a European run before – I was too young to have attended Terry Neill's side's runs in the 1970s and early 1980s.

Highbury was right on top of the players in contrast to the spacious home grounds of Torino and PSG. You could almost sense the life being crushed out of Torino in the quarter-final return-leg. Whatever defensive tactics they had Arsenal could match them. With no score in Italy the only Arsenal player with the guile to find a way past their defensive line up at Highbury was Paul Davis. He dropped a perfect free kick onto Tony Adams' head and the relief around the ground was staggering. It was suffocating stuff but memorable too because it showed just how George's side approached European games – like a game of footballing chess. One false move and Arsenal would've been dead, but somehow they prevailed.

Darren Epstein recalled both matches of the tie without fondness simply stating tongue in cheek that 'the best that can be said about those two games is boring!' Jem Maidment added,

The Torino home game was remarkably tense. They were a decent side with Benito Carbone latterly of Bradford, Sheffield Wednesday, Aston Villa and Andrea Silenzi up front (who later went to Nottingham Forest and failed badly).

I was in the east lower with my friend Chris and his dad John. Right at the back so you had to crane down to see the far side of the pitch. Chris had awful toothache so with that and the tense situation it wasn't an enjoyable experience. It was a tight game. It had to be Tony Adams who did the business. Funny really I was never his biggest fan, much to the clear annoyance and disgust of my mates, because I always felt he was quite a flawed player and those around him did not get the praise they deserved. However, he was a big game player and did the business when it mattered. That much is true. And he did that night. Also Paul Davis, coming to the end of his career, had a really great game too. Very underrated player was Davo.

The relief at the final whistle was something else. Strangers in the east stand leaving and shaking hands, hugging each other. Arsenal vs Torino under the floodlights at Highbury was an incredible night.

Dave Seager, author of acclaimed Arsenal book *Geordie Armstrong on the Wing* as well as the editor of the popular website *One-Nil-Down-Two-One-Up*, told me his memories of the night too,

Back then I was a young dad with another on the way and not too flush so my visits to Highbury were not as frequent as I would've liked. I did go to the home-leg of both the quarter-final vs Torino and the second-leg of the semi-final vs PSG. The home-leg of course is the game where *One-Nil-To-The-Arsenal* truly took hold [after being originally sung at the away game in Paris] and the atmosphere on both Highbury occasions was rocking. In truth the team offensively was struggling and in the league Arsenal were a shadow of the team who'd won the league only a few seasons earlier.

Deprived of the creative flair of Rocastle, Thomas and Limpar Arsenal had become a cup team. George Graham had lost none of his brilliance as a strategist and defensive coordinator and this was so evident in the run to European glory. Against Torino having drawn 0–0 with a resolute rear guard action in Turin we toiled at home until Tony Adams stole clear of his marker to glance a header in at the far post in the sixty-sixth minute. It was a tense last twenty-four minutes of course but I, among thousands, sang the team home for a 1–0 victory. In truth Arsenal were doing what Liverpool had done year after year in Europe. Keeping it incredibly tight away from home and then nicking the tie at home.

As someone who had a season ticket in the 'clock end' along with some old pals from school, university and friends through supporting our team I was always conscious of the away fans in the next block along.

At the time I used to pop down to Soccer Scene on Carnaby Street anytime I was in the West End. It was a real cult football shop back then and was peopled with knowledgeable staff and extremely unusual football shirts and paraphernalia. I remember going there a few days before the home leg against Torino to have a look around. As I flicked through the immaculate, high-quality football shirts from around the world I noticed the stylish Juventus top made by Kappa. It was how football kits should be: immediately recognisable, uncluttered and with traditional bold colouring. As I used to collect overseas football shirts I immediately thought to buy it and then it dawned on me as my mischievous side came out. I recall thinking how could I wind up the travelling Torino fans at our forthcoming match if I wore a Juventus shirt. Especially as news had come through that two Torino fans had been arrested for attempting to throw home-made bombs at us in Turin after the first leg. Arsenal being Arsenal, I love to think our response to that shocking news was far less violent and far more ironic and tongue in cheek.

Come the night, which was your average relatively chilly March evening in north London, I took my coat off at the start of the game and stood on my seat and faced the travelling hordes from Turin. My seat wasn't that far from the away-end and you could make out faces quite clearly and, as happened on many an occasion, actually mouth insults to a particular away fan who was even uglier than me. On this occasion when I hopped on my seat and caught the eye of a few Torino fans immediately the whole away-end went up in arms at the sight of an Arsenal fan in their hated rival's colours.

Don't ask me how I know it but *va fa cuolo* (go fuck yourself) was the preferred insult of choice from the purple clad visitors. All aimed at me. There were people practically foaming at the mouth hurling abuse at me, such was their hatred of Juventus. After Tony Adams scored early on I was up on my seat again with my Juventus shirt in full view of the, by now furious, away support. I could see a few doing throat-cutting gestures while others were throwing coins and lighters and anything else they could get their hands on which prompted the police to wade in and throw a few out.

As the game wore on, and the tension became unbearable, I forgot about the shirt until the relief at the final whistle. Whereupon I ran over to The Wiseman and Beaker, whose season tickets were lower down the clock nd, and jumped on a seat in full view of the gutted and angry Torino fans. It was a sight I'll never forget as more than 2,000 furious Torino fans and Ultras hurled abuse at me working themselves into an ever-more heightened frenzy. Looking back I'm not sure what I was thinking as it wouldn't have taken much for them to leap over into our end and come for me. Thankfully they didn't and I left after a smiling steward told me, 'get out before they go bonkers'. I looked at the steward and pointed to one bloke who was not only repeatedly undertaking throat-slicing movements that looked so theatrically preposterous at the speed and intensity he was carrying them out at it made him an object of utter ridicule, but screaming at me so hard his eyes were actually bulging. If he had been a cartoon character his eyes would have been on stalks. Both the steward and I looked on, mesmerised at his fury, as he then started kicking his chair in anger while tearing at his own scarf in what can only be described as a complete and utter loss of control. I then turned to the steward and replied with an ever bigger smile saying, 'Looks like they've done that already'.

As I walked down the exit to join a happy concourse full of Gooners my last sight was of the man being wrestled away by police in yellow jackets shining brightly against the north London night.

Dozens of Torino fans were ejected from the ground during the second-leg of the quarter-final of the European Cup Winners' Cup at Highbury which Arsenal won 1–0 to reach the semi-finals. The north London club will now play Paris St Germain.

Guardian, 20 March 1994.

7

PSG vs Arsenal: The Song is a Fairytale

European Cup Winners' Cup semi-final, first-leg. Paris Saint Germain 1 Arsenal 1.
3 April 1994.

> Where words fail, music speaks.
>
> > Hans Christian Andersen.

> (Together) We will make our plans.
>
> > 'Go West', The Pet Shop Boys.

> One-Nil-To-The-Arsenal
>
> > Arsenal fans, half-time at the Parc de Princes to the
> > tune of 'Go West' by the Pet Shop Boys.

It's the hands that give it away. The hands of a mechanic. Thick, stubby and honest. Working man's hands. That's the thing you first notice about Stephen Moszoro. Dad. Gooner. Working man. Stephen, or 'Mozzy' as he's known to his pals including the author who went to school with him in a down at heel part of London a long time ago. Father of two lovely girls. Long term Arsenal season ticket holder who has witnessed the majority of the club's triumphs (and crushing low points) over the last thirty or more seasons.

Over a pint in the Highbury Barn, itself a citadel of loyal Arsenal support by Mozzy, myself and countless other friends, he recalls our trip to Paris. He does this with an occasional rueful shake of the head but mostly with a smile. It's a smile only a fellow fan with knowledge of a riotous European away trip can understand. A smile saying 'how on earth did we manage that?' Holding his pint in those thick hands on a match-day, the dirt and the grime of his mornings work at the garage now proudly and meticulously washed off, he stands adjacent to me. To us. A crowd of friends who have seen it all following the Arsenal home and away matches. With a broad London accent Mozzy holds centre stage and talks of 'PSG away'.

Pointing one of those stubby fingers at me in mock anger and surprise he says, 'When I was sorting things out for that trip you told me we didn't need the AA European Breakdown cover as the car, my MK 3 82 Capri GL, got us up and down every motorway in the country with no faults at all! How wrong were you?' he asks the already laughing crowd of pals who know the story inside out but never tire of hearing it, as we all do of each other's European mishaps.

So I booked tickets for the Folkstone to Calais Seacat. A bit posh for us instead of a usual ferry. We didn't have any match tickets but that wasn't a problem as we planned to go out a day early before everyone else and buy some off touts. But five miles into France our xenophobic car decides to have a fit. Do you remember that bang? Still remember it like it was yesterday. That bang was us losing second and third gears.

The assembled crowd, eager to be entertained ahead of a home game laughs easily, with the fondness that comes from long-term friendship.

Do you remember the noise? You could hear us a mile off coming down the road? Police in the distance on the French motorways or whatever you call them could hear us coming. We could seem them staring at us in their parked cars. They were looking for us ages before they could see us. Then they clocked the Capri decked out in St George Crosses, Arsenal scarves tied out the window and all the bunting and what have you.

With a quick nod and a pause he adds, 'A bit like the Italian Job it was'. With the lads gripped in smiling silence Mozzy continues, 'So then we got to Paris in rush hour. Except we've now gone and lost first gear. Meaning we've only got fourth gear … with four big blokes and crates of beer. And then we lost fourth gear too.' The congregation erupts as asides are thrown back and forth as Mozzy looks on in mock indignation.

Do you remember having to push the car a mile through those narrow Paris streets to find a hotel? Course this was before the internet was invented and mobile phones so we never had a booking either. Eventually we found this underground car park, it was probably fitting we left the disabled car in a disabled parking bay.

So the next day, the first thing I do when I wake up with a hangover is to phone my brother Mark and get him to go to an AA shop and get breakdown cover for the car. I arranged for him to bring it out with him as we'd already planned to meet him under the Eiffel Tower at midday on the day of the game. He was due to get the train but he was late thanks to the typical French students having a demo about something or other on the railway line. We, on the other hand, headed up to the Parc de Princes to see if there were any touts but there was no joy.

Fed up, we went to the Champs Elysee for a wander with our beers and actually met a French tout outside the Virgin Megastore. He wanted stupid money for the tickets and even though we got him down a bit it was still pricey. Of course in those days we still had to cash cheques as we didn't have enough money on us. We messed him around a bit and he must have thought we were right amateurs but eventually we got enough dosh to pay him. Finally we headed up to the Eiffel Tower, again for a good drink from early afternoon, and met loads of other Gooners some of who we still see around. Including a lad called Captain Cod who's called that as he's always battered.

I look around at the faces who haven't heard the story before and I can see them slightly scoffing at the ridiculousness of it all. It's only because they didn't go through such memorable nonsense which bonded us all. As does any European trip for any set of fans. For Arsenal fans of a certain vintage that glorious European season was as memorable for its mishaps off the pitch as the memories created on it. Something those who never experienced it will never fully comprehend.

Mozzy continued with the surreal air post-match European evenings sometimes take on, 'So Mark turns up with all the documents and we're sorted. After the game –' before another train of thought derails him and forces him to choose another important memory 'didn't we go mental when Wrighty scored? Wasn't that the moment at half-time when 'One-Nil-to-the-Arsenal' started when they played that Pet Shop Boys song 'Go West'?' Everyone who was there nods in solemn acknowledgement, silently proud they were in attendance when such an important Arsenal anthem was born. With others who hadn't been there secretly wishing they had.

'Anyway, where was I?' he asked before another recollection jolts him back. 'Stewpot from Grange Hill! Do you remember we met Stewpot from Grange Hill in the Latin Quarter after the game?' The statement sounds as incongruous and surreal as it was. Because it was true, I was there too. We carried on drinking, singing, joking and laughing until daylight arrived all the while listening to Stewpot regale us with his plenty of stories from life on and off the set of Grange Hill. 'Next morning we had to sort out our recovery for the Capri. Do you remember me making all those 'Allo, 'Allo style accents? Not because I was taking the mickey but because I was trying to make them understand me better.' A voice pipes up, 'You didn't do a good job of it, you can't speak a word of French'.

Mozzy retorts, 'They didn't know that though did they?' Another voice chips in with, 'I bet they bloody did after listening to you'. Ignoring the laughter Mozzy explains, 'Anyway the truck turns up and only has two passenger seats for me and Layth so the Wiseman and Beaker couldn't get a lift back! They had to make their own way home. No money, no transport, they had bunked it all the way!' as good friends roar with laughter at the absurdity of it all. The absurdity of life on the road following The Arsenal abroad.

Matthew Bleasby, another PSG veteran from that trip, later concurs with the mechanic's story telling me with a warm smile,

That car of his. That bloody car! My favourite memory of the Paris trip was simply getting there. He'd literally gone through the gears since we'd got off the ferry at Calais to the extent we were noisily making our way down the Champs Elysées in fourth gear because that was the only one left working. We finally made the refuge of an underground car park and it limped into an empty spot. [...] It seems crazy to think we hadn't even booked anywhere to stay and were just carrying our bags and a crate of Fosters around central Paris in the expectation we'd simply come across a hotel which would take us.

I do remember the bloke on reception who, after checking us in and looking us up and down, said dryly, 'We do sell alcohol in Paris. You didn't have to take your own drink from London'. As if we were a bit slow and clueless ... which I suppose we were back then! Before we found that hotel however an animated local came along pointing out we couldn't park in that spot in the car park. As I can speak a bit of French I helped with the subsequent conversation. 'What's he saying' Mozzy kept asking me. With all of us a bit tired and irritable I replied matter-of-factly, 'He says you can't park there, Mozz it's a disabled spot'. Mozzy then turned around and said, with all the exasperation of a driver with a car that doesn't work, replied in a high-pitched London accent, 'Well facking tell 'im the cars' facking disabled an all', before walking off with his crate of fourty-eight cans. To be fair to Mozzy he'd earned a drink after getting us there ...

We were in Paris three days before the game and still managed to miss kick-off. It was a great atmosphere in the Parc de Princes and we're all proud of being part of the Arsenal choir which originally started the whole 'One-Nil-to-the-Arsenal' that of course spawned a myriad of songs all over the country. It started at half-time when the announcer started playing 'Go West' by the Pet Shop Boys as part of their half-time music. During the 'Go West' bit, a few fans started singing 'One-Nil' and pointing to the PSG fans to our left. Gradually more and more joined in and by the time the song had finished the whole away-end was singing 'One-Nil' as a sea of arms pointed to the increasingly annoyed PSG fans. It just evolved over the second-half to, 'One-Nil-To-The-Arsenal' and despite a PSG equaliser it stuck as the anthem of the campaign. I do remember the DJ for the final in Copenhagen seemed to play 'Go West' on loop as the pre-match to get the fans going, although by then we didn't need much prompting.

London taxi driver, long-time Arsenal season ticket holder and good friend Nigel Maitland recalls PSG away in his own inimitable way. He told me,

Patient Paul did the driving again via the ferry, we had decided not to do the silly Kent village drinking thing we had done for Liège this time, and we arrived at the

Hotel Lunar (Looney we called it) Park in the centre of Paris early on the morning of the game. Paul, me and Dave were this time accompanied by Paul's brother, Sean, who came as substitute for Micky who had broken his leg playing football the previous weekend.

After a few beers we met up with the bikers Ollie and Mark. Ollie had managed to get three tickets in the PSG end. We agreed that Ollie, Mark and Dave would have the tickets and that me, Paul and Sean would try our luck outside the ground. To that end the three of us went to the Parc des Princes (or Parc de Ponces we called it mid-afternoon). On the way we went into one of Paris' finest weapon/knife shops. The array of flick knives, CS gas canisters was both fascinating and unnerving at the same time.

When we got to the ground we saw a couple of Arsenal fans being set upon by about half a dozen PSG blokes. We went over to explain to them the error of their ways and out of nowhere came another twenty or so of the enemy. Bearing in mind what we had just seen in the weapon shop we were anticipating a bit of a hiding we just 'explained' to as many as we could as quickly as we could. To our amazement they suddenly all turned and ran away. We yelled 'be off with you' (or words to that effect) but my personal joy/relief was short lived as a riot policeman's baton smashed into the back of my knee. We now understood why all the PSG hooligans had fucked off. The Robocop's were actually quite restrained overall as there was only three of us, the two Arsenal fans we had initially tried to help had long since vanished (cheers). Paul however had sustained a nasty head injury and was covered in blood. The chief Robocop was talking to Paul and I must admit I lost it a bit and was ranting (a mixture of booze, relief and adrenalin always works). Anyway they eventually released us and advised us to go away from the ground. Paul later told me that he had told the chief Robocop that we had had our tickets nicked by the PSG mob and he was considering getting us into the ground but changed his mind when he saw me going mental.

Que sera, sera. We staggered round Paris trying to find a bar that would serve us, admittedly we looked a bit of a sight, and eventually found a run-down bar in a less than salubrious area full of what looked like extras from *Les Miserables* who gave us a less than welcoming look. When we looked at the telly we saw that Arsenal were winning 1–0 and everything seemed ok. Unfortunately, by the time we'd ordered the beers PSG had equalised. I can't remember much after that but woke up in The Hotel Looney Park glad to be in one piece (sort of) and with one foot in the Cup Winners Cup Final.

The journey home was again uneventful (well you can only have so much fun) although I do remember stopping off at a service station supermarket to get some beers. The trouble was that they were warm so some bright spark (me probably) saw some ice on one of the empty frozen/refrigerated counters and covered the beers with it. It was only when we got into the confines of the motor that we realised the ice must have come from the fish counter. I think we were too battered and tired to care and, to be quite honest, I think I would rather have cold fishy beer than warm beer. That's what I was trying to convince everyone on the long journey home anyway.

Gooner editor Kevin Whitcher also remembered the trip and match,

Arsenal were in the semi-finals of the Cup Winners' Cup, would we get holders Parma? Benfica again? Or Paris St Germain? It turned out, of course, to be the latter with a visit to France for the first-leg. I used the opportunity to treat my then girlfriend, who just happened to speak decent French, to a romantic break.

We didn't have tickets, but she was able to sort a pair from a local bar the day before the game. Such things can endear a girl to your heart. Anyhow, it was chaos on the day of the game with running battles between the Boulogne Boys (the PSG ultras) and the Arsenal fans. A large group of the latter were herded up at one point and put in vehicles and told they would be given safe passage to the away entrance. In fact they were taken to what was basically a cow shed miles outside the centre until the game had finished. Fortunately we avoided this and we took our excellent seats at pitch-side a few rows in front of a large block of Arsenal fans who had presumably bought tickets from one of the travel agents who arranged tour deals including match tickets. It was a cracking game and one that saw the birth of the 'One-Nil-to-the-Arsenal' chant to the strains of 'Go West'. The PSG fans were singing something to the tune blasted out over the public address system. I can't recall what and probably never even understood it at the time either but the memory is clear of the away supporters adapting it when the Gunners went 1–0 up courtesy of Ian Wright, and the rest is history.

PSG were a very good team in the making and Arsenal were by no means clear favourites for this tie. They were on their way to becoming French champions that season and would reach the Champions League last four only twelve months later. They'd eliminated Real Madrid in the quarter-finals and their team featured the likes of David Ginola and George Weah, Brazilian international Valdo and some very experienced domestic names, like Paul Le Guen and Daniel Bravo. They were no pushovers and equalized in the first-leg to set up a highly charged tense return at Highbury.

Mike Francis, *Gooner* publisher added,

I opted to play safe for my first European adventure and booked to go with the Arsenal Travel Club who chartered a plane into one of the Paris airports. I vividly recall the plane coming to a halt in a remote part of the airfield alongside a tank. Clearly English football fans were still treated with utmost caution by our hosts. Such was the gendarmes' paranoia that we would wreak havoc in their city that we were bussed straight from the airport to the stadium, where we were individually searched before being permitted entry at least two hours before kick-off. No opportunity to take in any sights although I did just about manage to catch a glimpse of the Eiffel Tower as we made our way round the ring-road.

The game lives in my memory for two reasons. Firstly, the birth of what became 'our' chant at half-time which we were able to sing thanks to a typically opportunist strike by Ian Wright in the first-half and the decision of the stadium DJ to play the Pet Shop Boys track 'Go West'. Unfortunately, our lead didn't last long into the second-half as PSG equalised through David Ginola. I recall watching the home fans at the far end of the ground surge towards the front of their enclosure in celebration. It was nothing I hadn't seen before and been part of on the old north bank but then I remembered we were in an all-seater stadium and a mass of people clambering over seats like that was likely to leave a few Parisians sporting bruises the following morning. Ouch!

Arsenal shareholder Darren Epstein recalled it to me like this:

PSG, now that was a draw. When it was made everyone went mad. The PSG fans had, in those days, a terrible reputation and I didn't want to be in the away-end. My friends' aunt lived in Paris and went to HMV to buy tickets for the game for me and four of us ended up right next to the director's box in the main stand. That was the first game since we returned to play in Europe where I really felt like we were at a game with atmosphere. The crowd was a sight to see, something that I'd always seen on TV when they showed foreign teams, noise, flares, smoke – it was very loud.

PSG were really good, and Ginola was their star. We were linked with him around that time and he really put a performance in at the Parc de Princes. The game ended. There was no security stopping us going over to the director's area and we just walked into the director's lounge. David Dein laughed when he saw me, I knew him well at that time and he didn't tell anyone – we ended up chatting to all the dignitaries. I walked out with a commemorative bottle of champagne! Of course it was also the game when 'One-Nil-To-The-Arsenal' was born. The PSG announcer played it at half-time and Arsenal fans started to accommodate the words to our song. The thing about 'One-Nil-To-The-Arsenal' is that so many who weren't around then or who barely reported on us think it was because we were boring and scored single goals to win the game – it was nothing of the kind. The Arsenal team from 1989 to 1993 was expansive, open and very attacking, something people forget. But when we went one-nil up we rarely lost the game, that's where it really comes from, not the fact we scored few goals. When we went one-nil up, you pretty much knew what the outcome was.

Parisians, and passionate Paris Saint Germain fans, Antoine de Servigny and Thibaud Mounier were at that momentous semi-final game at the Parc de Princes too. In perfect English they recounted their memories to me,

In 1994 we really believed it was our year to win our first European trophy. The PSG team had never been so strong, a team made up of Brazilian and French players. Before playing Arsenal we beat the great Real Madrid in our best ever game with a 4–1 last minute victory at home after the away game had been lost 3–1.

At this time Arsène wasn't there and nor were the Quatarians either for PSG. Arsenal didn't frighten us at that time even if our track record wasn't good against

English teams. In the end PSG had never been in a position to qualify for the final. The Arsenal players were cool, full of confidence, and scored in both games to knock us out. During the first-leg game in Paris when Ian Wright sent kisses to the Parisian supporters after he scored even the whistles and insults had no effect on him. On the contrary, it motivated the Arsenal players even more. Ginola, our idol, equalized but even a draw wasn't good enough before playing away in the second-leg at Highbury. Unfortunately in the streets surrounding our stadium, the Parc des Princes, there were some fights between violent supporters.

Even David Ginola was quoted at the time as saying, 'In Paris our concern was that there shan't be any hooliganism. Our gangs don't come to watch the game they come to fight and that can be a problem.'

Anglophile Antoine, mirroring the traditional respect French football fans in general have for Arsenal Football Club, added on a more positive note,

> Thanks to our new international stars, PSG is back and hopefully will be able again to compete with the best European teams.
>
> We hope we get a possible revenge to Arsenal, a team that is fully respected and admired in Paris. We beat Chelsea in 2015 much to the delight of our supporters, and no doubt Arsenal supporters too, maybe we can beat Arsenal in 2016!

The good-natured and knowledgeable Antoine and his friend Thibaud were absolutely right, the Arsenal team of 1993/94 were gaining in confidence in every round.

The morning after the game France's respected national sports newspaper *L'Equipe* carried a lovely cameo of what it must have been like to be a player in that game, deliciously reporting on various exchanges between the flamboyant Ginola and Arsenal defenders. Bearing in mind flamboyant wide-men were hardly our renowned back four's list of favourite people. *L-Equipe*: 'Ginola's English lesson'.

David Ginola cracks up. He recalls in English with a Toulannais accent,

> During the whole match Dixon, Adams and Bould didn't stop insulting me, 'Fuck you, fuck you!' they screamed at me. From the first moment I told myself, 'This can't be true, I'm dreaming, this is not the English …' And then in the fourty-eighth minute David scored a header. His response, also stinging, did not suffice. He ran towards Bould and cried just as strongly, 'Fuck you, Fuck you asshole!'
>
> At the end of the match, this did not however prevent the two men from exchanging shirts. That must be what you call fair-play.

Alan Smith tells me, 'I suppose when we got past PSG we started thinking we might have a chance, you start thinking you might be in with a shout. When you look back they had a fantastic defence.' He takes another sip of his coffee, looks me squarely in the eye and simply replies with a modest but utterly heartfelt pride, 'I was very proud of all the boys' performances that night'.

Stewart Houston recalls the night, after I mention the fact PSG were a quality team who would reach the quarter-finals of the Champions League the next season, by saying,

They were a top side you're right Layth. I remember this tie, but for me at the time and looking back this was one of those matches where it was all about the result.

It was so big. This game was massive in our campaign. It was just all about getting to the final, hook, line and sinker, our feeling was 'We just need to get through to the final'. That's all it's about because we've come so far down the line and it was really about digging out a result, to get over the line to get to the final.

They always used to say FA Cup semi-finals are never special, it was all about getting to the final, and this was very much the case against Paris. There's almost no greater disappointment than losing in a semi-final. If you lose in a final of course it's disappointing, but at least you can look back and say you reached a showpiece final even if you didn't win it. Not that you want that of course, and it's not a case of settling for second best, but at least you're in the final. But with a semi-final, well there's nothing like that. You're out after coming so far with absolutely nothing to show for it.

I tell him I was in the away end that night with my friends and went bonkers when Wrighty scored with that header before asking him what he did when the goal went in, and how important did he think his goal was?

In a low deep voice, with real feeling, he answers,

That away goal was paramount. No question about it. When you get to that stage the margins are much, much smaller, if you've come from playing Odense to play a crack French side in the semi-final then the margins are so small – everything counts. And that away goal by Wrighty was absolutely crucial for us. The ratios have to be so high. You're going to get far less chances against a top team like PSG, where you might get five or six chances against Odense. You might even maybe have just one or two chances over the two legs in fact.

Stewart, his voice passionate and serious, adds with intensity, 'and you've got to be able to put them away'.

Patrick Barclay added recalled the night in his inimitable way to me,

Paris Saint Germain, Arsenal's opponents in the European Cup Winners' Cup semi-final, as you know Layth, were not of the calibre or moneyed-force to be reckoned with as they are now. Although they did have players like David Ginloa. The Parc de Princes is one of those stadiums where the spectators are a way from the pitch, but the atmosphere generated was still good.

PSG did have a good team at that time, Ginola, Paul le Guen, Rai, Weah, all wonderfully elegant players. I think in most of the games Arsenal played on that run they would never be mistaken for technical maestros on show. A lot of the teams Arsenal faced would have had far greater technicians so Arsenal were definitely the more workmanlike side in the games leading up to the final, and of course the final itself, which was ultimately the last hurrah of the George Graham era.

In the lead-up to the match David Ginola told English journalists somewhat dismissively,

You chauvinists, you English, you remain closed in your little world and you learn nothing that way. We know all about the championships of other countries because we know they are as good as ours. But the English? Oh no. You don't open your eyes or your spirits to anything beyond your shores. I may be able to take advantage of the fact no-one has heard of me. Actually it makes me a little sad. But even if the English don't know me, I shall be there. And I am looking forward to introducing myself.

That night, so were our defenders.

PSG had conceded a miserly fifteen goals in thirty-one league games and they looked strong defensively as well as offensively with Valdo, Le Guen, Guerin, Weah and Ginola liable to threaten at any moment. But Arsenal were gaining in confidence all the time on that run. They had also just clinched St Totteringham's Day back in England the weekend before with a 1–0 victory over Liverpool – which saw my friends and I stay out all night in Camden before getting into Mozzy's Capri first thing the next morning and drive to Paris.

A bullish George Graham said on the eve of the game, 'They're better going forward than Torino and they get a lot of movement from midfield. And they've got a great defence … but,' he added almost as much as a threat as an observation, 'I don't think it's been tested week in week out'.

Alan Smith began as what could be interpreted as a lone striker on the night, but was anything but. The crucial point tactically, which was missed by many, was in only having a single front man as Stewart Houston explained to me. Was the fact that the forward, Smith, was actually in the middle of an attacking triumvirate with support from his two wide forwards, Wright and Merson. He also had the menace of midfielders on the night Selley and Jensen, as well as from two energetic full-backs who looked to exploit space in the lines between PSGs midfield and defence, namely Winterburn and Dixon.

Even David Lacey of *The Guardian*, who to be fair knew tactics inside out, was effusive when writing the morning after about George Graham and his side's performance.

In his report entitled 'Arsenal Stroll in the Parc' he wrote,

Arsenal left Paris last night feeling entitled to stroll along the *Bois de Boulogne* with an independent air. Such was their performance in holding Paris St Germain to 1–1 in the opening leg of the Cup Winners' Cup semi-finals that only the flintiest of hearts would have denied George Graham's team the privilege.

In no way were Arsenal boring or predictable last night. They took on the French League's runaway leaders and their Brazilians in a fast, open game of counter attack, and over the ninety minutes looked the better team.

With Ian Wright scoring the crucial away goal thirty-five minutes in, meeting a Davis cross from the right and directing his heading low inside Lama's left-hand post, it sent my friends and myself into paroxysms of joy. It transpired into the archives too as we would later discover we were captured on ITV's match coverage – my parents still have the video tape of it. Indeed my dad went through a stage of telling everyone he met that his son was on ITV which left a fair few thinking my dad had an offspring working for a national television channel. Despite Ginola meeting a cross swung in from the Brazilian Valdo in the fourty-eighth minute and drawing on all their defensive discipline and physical and mental strength, Wright's away goal meant the team could look forward to the second-leg knowing a sterling defensive performance and a single goal was all we needed to progress to a European final.

All we would need in the second-leg at Highbury, it transpired, was simply: 'One-Nil-To-The-Arsenal.'

8

Arsenal vs PSG: The Happy Family or The Ugly Duckling

European Cup Winners' Cup, semi-final, second-leg. Arsenal 1 Paris Saint Germain 0 (Arsenal won 2-1 on aggregate). 12 April 1994.

But a mermaid has no tears, and therefore she suffers so much more.
Hans Christian Andersen, *The Little Mermaid*.

Highbury could become the cemetery of Parisian delusions.
L'Equipe, 31 March 1994.

The club's history is all about winning trophies. It's all or nothing tonight. We respond to that sort of challenge. We can't go and worry about bookings.
George Graham, Arsenal programme notes, Highbury. 12 April 1994.

Paris, Highbury awaits you. Welcome to Highbury the Home of Football.

Although they will pass under this banner on entering the stadium, it's a totally different welcome that will await the Parisians in thirteen days' time in London. The streets are back to back with terraced houses more grey brick than red, then suddenly round a bend in the pavement, Highbury. Four English stands. High, cornered, spilling forth their last spectators to vent their breath on the touch line.

No fences, and often a chorus for ninety minutes accompanying the efforts of eleven typically in red and white with a cannon embroidered on their hearts. Here is the scene.

For the scenario, the actors already have a clear idea of what awaits them for this match of guaranteed suspense. On one side 'the Frenchies', Artur Jorge, the mute, Joël Bats, the James Bond of PSG, they've come to breathe in the atmosphere of this popular area of north-east London to discover the home style of play of eleven English who have previously undertaken a slightly different journey.

Arsenal, its certain will not close down the game under the pretext that they'll take the score. But it's unlikely that the English will repeat the blunder of two seasons ago when having successfully drawn 1–1 at Benfica, they were beaten by an assault of Portuguese goals, exploding their rear guard by an unfortunate goal before being beaten by a team able to control the ball.

'We are going to press them, we have learned our lesson', explains Graham, 'From now on we are going to regard patience as a virtue'. John Jensen is not so convinced by this option, 'Paris must work out how to score. From our side, encouraged by our crowd, it will be difficult to resist the temptation not to push forward. I think it is reasonable to believe that we have the quality to impose ourselves at home. It's certainly not going to be easy but I think at 1–1 we have a great chance to progress to the final.

On the game plan Graham is going to have to harness this will to play, but everyone who regularly watch Arsenal in England promise a team slightly different in structure and style of play from the one that came to draw the match at the *Parc* on Tuesday night. We'll have to see if the same eleven start in the 4-3-3 formation and only perhaps the tempo will be a fraction speedier as a result of the pressing of 39,000 Gunners fans.

From his bench, George Graham perfectly notes that, 'Paris were cramped by our ability to maintain a pace altogether. The French were not visibly used to playing at such a high speed over ninety minutes. They would do well to prepare for this type of match in the return-leg'.

Paul Merson said as much, 'It's necessary to work hard in training, that's the key to success.'

Graham concludes, 'The Parisians are used to facing strong pressure for twenty to thirty minutes per match, but at Highbury they are going to have to maintain an infernal pace for the whole match. Without so much as mentioning their covering of ground, which was so perfect at the Parc, and the defensive base so dear to the Scottish manager.

It will depend after all on Arsenal achieving a maximum of corners and set pieces around Lama's penalty area. They'll find themselves well placed with the great oaf of a defence (Adams, Bould) the vision of Smith or the menace Wright, to repeat the success of the Parc.

Highbury could become the cemetery of Parisian delusions.'

L'Equipe – Thursday 31 March 1994.

[The picture to accompany the preview showed Ginola surrounded by our steadfast defenders, with the caption reading, 'Ginola isolated and beaten by the windmill of Winterburn and Bould, an image too typical of the first-leg at Parc de Princes. It will be necessary for Paris to play closer if they are going to survive at Highbury.']

With thanks to Guy Wiseman.

One thing I always used to love about new signings unfamiliar with Arsenal at Highbury was when they would talk about the day they put pen to paper with the club. They would of course talk in gushing terms about the fact they'd always wanted to play for the Gunners (some I even believed). They'd habitually mention the fighting spirit, the great fans, the history and tradition, *ad nasuem*, so much so that you could almost hear the scripted lines the player's agent had written for them. But what I always looked out for was the ones who would regale the assembled journalists with a genuine sense of wonder about physically arriving at the club.

For example, I immediately warmed to Manu Petit when he spoke in hushed reverence of the day he arrived outside the Marble Halls in Avenell Road in a black taxi. The fact the vehicle came straight from N17 and a meeting Tottenham's Alan Sugar, and getting the Lilywhites to pay for the cab too was full of satisfying irony. It was when he spoke of that first sight of Highbury that I knew we had a player who would savour playing for our beloved institution.

He said in truthful wonder, 'All I could see on my journey were houses and streets, and I thought to myself where is Arsenal? And then, as we drove into another street full of houses there it appeared, from nowhere, this magnificent stadium in the middle of all the houses. It was amazing. Beautiful even.'

There's a famous black and white picture of a packed Highbury under floodlights as the team played Scottish giants Rangers in the early 1950s. I have a print of it and even now on busy mornings in a house full of children about to go to school, with my partner about to start work for the day and with me getting ready to head to the newspaper I work for, it still stops me dead in my tracks.

For the sight of a full Arsenal Stadium under lights – to give it its proper name – is one that, as Manu Petit described with such reverence, is beautiful. Occasionally in the frenzied anticipation of the heady moments before an evening kick-off at Highbury for big games on cold misty nights, I would actually get a rush of goose-bumps at the sight as I rushed up the steps to claim my place in the clock-end.

The fact you are immediately met by a loud guttural roar from a passionate crowd as it rolls round that famous old ground which is packed to the rafters only adds to your sensory anticipation. Although the photograph I am looking at is in black and white it stirs an image of the brightest green football pitch you have ever seen. The stage set for your heroes perfectly illuminated by bright floodlights on a black, cold north London night that you can even see the sheen on the pitch that the brilliance of the bulbs highlights. Immediately you're transported back to important matches at the evocative old ground loved by so many as you walk down those same streets a myriad of Arsenal players would've travelled on their way to signing for our beloved institution. The smell of the onions from the burger vans whose bitter black offerings were always of dubious repute, as indeed were many of those hawkers. You hear the cries of the craggy-faced programme sellers, resplendent in white jackets, isolated but vociferous, aggressively proficient as they thrust a programme at you without ceremony, more concerned with keeping the queues down. For there never seemed to be enough of those wonderfully unemotional men who knew their Arsenal when you came trotting down Avenell Road towards the clock-end turnstiles just ahead of kick-off.

If these taciturn programme sellers were still offering their wares you knew you hadn't overdone your pre-match drinking. For me to go through the turnstiles without a programme to purchase somehow diminished the game for me. Which would always disrupt the next home game for me as I searched for the errant missing programme from Jack Kelsey's homely little shop I always thought was more akin to a newsagents than a football club.

Another reason I am still slightly bemused when marketing people tell me Arsenal are a 'global brand' is because I feel like saying to them, 'I don't suppose you remember Jack taking the time to put a big black cross with a large indelible marker on every cup final voucher in every programme to prevent touts from buying them up in a desperate attempt to qualify for cup final tickets ahead of loyal supporters?'

Arsenal has always been a big club, but equally, the egalitarian nature of Highbury always reminded you of a homely feel. I recall those programme sellers from our past, flogging the 'programme and handbook' from what I believed to be hand painted wooden crates with wheels. The sight of them wheeling one away after selling out their stock was reminiscent of a meat or fish porter in one of London's famed but long-gone markets. The sight of these craggy faced men scurrying away to get into the ground is in contrast to the legions of fresh faced young programme selling staff at The Emirates today. These youngsters, planted no doubt strategically, outside a myriad of points are as timid and uninterested as those old timers who cared about the club were knowledgeable and passionate. Then again I doubt the old timers knew much about zero-hours contracts, or stewarding companies paying less than the living wage.

The men were a nice personal touch in an age before corporate logos took over, and while we're talking about programmes who remembers the club advertising for fans to help paint the stadium over the summer in return for a 'terrace season ticket'? So, programme in hand as fried onions waft past, you walk down Avenell Road. At the top of Avenell Road all you see is a mass of humanity. Red and white humanity. In the distance you can see hordes of people milling around the steps to the famed marble halls. But you know as kick off approaches there's no reason to be there as the teams are already in the dressing rooms. Unless, like me before one notorious north London derby one of your players comes rushing out to place a large white envelope full of tickets into a well-known tout's hand before the tout thrust a brown envelope full of used twenty pound notes into my heroes hand. A hero I never looked at in the same way again.

The low level dressing rooms are part of the enthralling art deco east stand. The same ones which had the unheard of splendour and opulence of famous heated floors in the depressed 1930s, even as George Orwell wrote *The Road to Wigan Pier*. The same dressing rooms immortal legends hung out of celebrating trophy wins.

You look up at the east stand briefly because it is beautiful, tastefully lit against the night sky, before you take your place in the swaying queue outside the clock-end turnstiles.

You know it's a big game because there are police horses attempting crowd control. Yet it was a gripe of many that Arsenal fans could be relied on to police themselves outside turnstiles, and the mounted constabulary's presence only seemed to add bad humour and resentment not to mention a crush at times as the aloof and hard-hearted riders shouted at fans they were corralling needlessly. You then carefully tear your season ticket cup tie voucher and hand it to the turnstile gateman behind red metal wire and you briefly enter his world which is an arcane but precise arrangement in dealing with paper tickets, and push through timeless Victorian turnstiles, clicking reassuringly. You silently breathe a sigh of relief you are now inside Highbury, as you prepare to support your team through ninety minutes of pained emotions, knowing all at once you are powerless in influencing the result but also as a combined mass of 38,000 supporters equally as capable of swaying a referees decision. Or intimidating a callow and unwary young player into making a crucial mistake, or simply fuelling your heroes onto greater heights imaginable, through the sheer noise of fanatical support. You can hear the overexcited tones of the announcer mangle the names of the continental opposition as you rush through that crowded thoroughfare under the clock-end and climb the steps to your block.

Occasionally in the frenzied anticipation of the heady moments before an evening kick-off at Highbury for big games on cold misty nights, I would actually get a rush of goosebumps at the sight as I rushed up the steps to claim my place in the clock end. The fact you are immediately met by a loud guttural roar from a passionate crowd as it rolls round that famous old ground which is packed to the rafters only adds to your sensory anticipation. Although it is a dark night you come across the brightest, greenest football pitch you have ever seen. The stage set for your heroes perfectly illuminated by bright lights on a pitch black, cold north London night that you can even see the sheen on the pitch that the brilliance of the bulbs highlights. And you realise Manu Petit was right: Highbury was beautiful. And nowhere was more beautiful, in memory, than the night we played Paris Saint Germain in the semi-final second-leg of the 1993/94 European Cup Winners' Cup Final.

There had never been any doubt through the course of the 1993/94 season that Paris Saint Germain would be champions of France. Perennial rivals Marseille had fallen far from grace after winning the 1993 Champions League with Arsene

Wenger's Provencal nemesis Bernard Tapie's match fixing scandals being exposed. Even if critics from outside the capital sneered at a lack of flamboyance from Artur George's side, the fact was that they were far too consistent and defensively sound encourages *les autres*. But if, as the respected national sportspaper *L-Equipe* wrote ahead of the first-leg, it was a 'night for men' then this hugely important second leg at a throbbing Highbury needed to be an evening for cool heads, on the pitch at least. But even *The Guardian's* David Lacey, never a man to fail to put the boot into the Gunners if he had the chance, appeared to be swept up in the fervour for an English team to qualify for a European final after the fallow post-Heysel years. In his preview of the second-leg, prophetically headlined 'Cautious Gunners Looking to be Quick on the Draw', he wrote, 'For once even Arsenal's sternest critics would not begrudge George Graham's pragmatists another goalless draw at Highbury tonight'. Everyone at Highbury that night knew a clean sheet would see Arsenal through. But no home side in the tournament so far had managed to keep a clean sheet against the Parisians who had impressively triumphed 1-0 over the Spanish aristocrats of Real Madrid in the Bernabeu stadium in the opening leg of the previous round.

Did George Graham make his team watch the video nasty of their era-defining 3-1 humbling at the hands of a vibrant counter attacking Benfica side in the 1991/92 European Cup? If so, they could've easily substituted Wenger's Monegasque Liberian protégé George Weah (now plying his trade in the French capital) and the Brazilian Valdo, for the waspish game changer Isias of the Portuguese giants in terms of players to fear. As Graham said at the time, 'They are very dangerous away from home. I think we surprised them over there. Maybe they underestimated us. They could well play better at Highbury than they did in Paris.' On the threat of David Ginola, Graham added pointedly in his managerial style which drew comparisons with Manchester United's Alex Ferguson, 'Ginola's an excellent player, but I hope we don't see him diving about so much this time'.

Another issue on Graham's mind, and surely the players too, was the fact the squad had eight men on a yellow card including: John Jensen, Tony Adams, Paul Merson, Ian Selly and ominously Ian Wright. They were painfully aware that another caution would see them miss any potential final. Graham, as was his habit of downplaying problems to ease pressure on his men spoke nonchalantly on the matter before the game saying, 'It's part and parcel of European football. You get yellows cards for innocuous, unimportant things. We can't go out worrying about bookings.' Lacey, astute as ever in his writing added, 'Nevertheless it would be foolish for Ian Wright to pick up a booking'.

When Stewart Houston spoke of that immortal Highbury night during our interview what struck me as he spoke to me was the sense of admiration in his voice for Ian Wright and his utter respect for him not only as a player, but as a man too.

When I asked him what he remembered most about the game that evening he gave me an interesting reply, one which echoed the sense of it being Arsenal against the world and the resulting *espirit de corps* it generated. A feeling engendered by the fact it wasn't only players and managers who felt sometimes the club attracted undue criticism, for the fans already knew that more than anyone. As Stewart Houston told me perceptively,

Paul Gascoigne won acclaim for crying after he was booked in the semi-final vs Germany in Italia 1990 which would have seen him miss the final, but I thought Ian Wright after the initial shock kept his head after being booked more for the overreaction than the foul itself.

Like you say Layth, Gazza won plaudits for crying and Ian was a highly emotional type of guy, so I could understand him going 'Shit, I know we're going to go through but I won't be on the pitch. And it must have been horrible to imagine, it does happen of course and it is part of the game, but you feel so badly for him. He played such a crucial part all through the campaign and then he gets booked and knows he'll be the unlucky one and won't be there for the final in Copenhagen.

I have to say I thought he acted so very professionally that night. His attitude was exemplary. It was a very big thing to carry on after the initial shock and play for the team and his teammates knowing he would miss any final. It was a mark of the man for him to do that. I think he showed great character in doing that.

He was one of those characters Wrighty, when he was criticised or when things weren't going his way he would think 'I'll bloody show you'. He dug in deep. He got a lot of credit that night for the way he finished the game in my opinion. He was mentally tough. Very, very tough. Whether it was his south London background or the fact he had to wait a lot longer than he would have wanted to break into league football I don't know. But there was a terrific mental strength and toughness about him that always came out, but more so than ever after he got booked on the night knowing he'd miss the final.

He won a lot of respect that night for the character he showed.

And as Stewart Houston, a tough but fair football man who loves the game and Arsenal Football Club as much as anyone, finished the sentence I could almost hear his voice catching in admiration and respect of Ian Wright, as well as the memory of that incredible Gunners team and their refusal to be beaten. And it makes me proud to be a Gooner.

It is interesting that the legendary Patrick Barclay told me twenty-one years on that he couldn't recall the match too vividly, but he was struck by how tense the latter stages were, even from the Highbury press box.

It was such an important game and the longer the match went on the more it became clear to everyone at Highbury just how critical it was for Arsenal not to concede.

I touched on the fact in my *Observer* newspaper column on the Sunday before the crucial second-leg tie, along with a few perceptive quotes from Alan Smith.

I hear you interviewed him for your book. Please pass on my best to him. Not only was he a vastly underrated player but he is a good man, and good journalist. Someone I have a lot of time and respect for.

I simply replied to the great Paddy Barclay, 'For what it's worth, I completely agree with what you say about him as a player. And having met him in person I couldn't agree more with him being a decent man.' Paddy, ever generous, added graciously, 'If you can find my piece in the archives you're more than welcome to use it'. One trip to the British Library later, here's Paddy's exceptional Paris Saint Germain preview piece reproduced in full with Mr Barclay's kind consent.

Characteristically incisive and analytical it's also instructive, he notes Arsenal's traditional habit of finishing seasons strongly. Plus ça change and all that.

The idea that English clubs, upon returning to European competition after the post-Heysel ban, would resume their domination of the Champions' Cup has proved more than a little vain. Not once, in attempts by Arsenal, Leeds and Manchester United, have they even survived the winter cut. But the Cup Winners' Cup has offered encouragement, and on Tuesday night Arsenal ought to follow United's example in 1991 by reaching the final. Whether they can actually win it, as United did when Mark Hughes finished off a supine Barcelona, is another matter. Parma, the holders, or Benfica lie in wait for George Graham's team if, having comfortably held Paris St Germain to 1–1 in the Parc de Princes, they complete the task at Highbury. First things first, though, and the French in their current mood are beatable. The spring that went out of their step in the first-leg had not returned last Tuesday at Nantes, where they suffered their first defeat in twenty-eight league matches. Nor is tiredness likely to be alleviated by the inferiority complex French clubs tend to carry into contests with the English, whom they seldom overcome.

Arsenal, meanwhile, can take heart from a habit of finishing seasons strongly: last year they won both domestic cups, the year before their last defeat was on 29 January and the year before that they lost only once after 2 February. Graham, often criticised for changing his team frequently, may argue that he is simply recognising the reality of the modern game's physical and mental demands. The main danger to their European ambition may lie, as it did when Torino came to Highbury in the previous round, in their own flat patch which puts both the Stadio delle Alpi and the Parc de Legumes to shame. If the visitors are once again refreshed by the sort of surface professional footballers ought to be able to take for granted, Arsenal may need the patience that kept Torino at bay before Tony Adams's header settled the tie; and this time they know 0–0 would suffice.

Of course they had the same comfort when Benfica visited Highbury in the Champions' Cup in 1991, and lost 3–1 after extra time, but Arsenal are beginning to show signs of a European education tempering 'gung-ho' approach, as Graham called it, that contributed to their downfall then. Far from being fooled by their ten goal aggregate thrashing of Standard Liège early in this campaign, they have taken a calmer attitude into subsequent challenges and, thus far, put scarcely a foot wrong.

It is a little early to say that, just as travel broadened Liverpool's minds in the 70s, Arsenal might derive lasting benefit from exposure to styles more thoughtful than the mainstream English power play of which they are rightly regarded as symbolic. But Graham has adjusted cleverly to Europe and it is significant that the thirty-two year-old Paul Davis, often neglected at home despite the fact that careful passing is his principal attribute, has taken a significant role in the team's progress. So too has the thirty-one year-old Alan Smith, that perennially underrated centre-forward. With Davis and Smith, the side has fewer rough edges.

'It's not so much that we've purposely gone out to change our game in Europe', says Smith, 'more that it's happened naturally. With opponents standing off you can knock the ball around. The back four can take their time and give it to the midfield, which suits Paul because he can direct things. But a big difference is that we've all learned from the Benfica defeat. We thought we'd done the hard work over there, we took the lead – and then they hit us. I think that experience stood us in good stead against Torino.'

One more night of maturity and Arsenal should be in their third European final. They won the Fairs Cup in 1970. Ten years later, Valencia's goalkeeper denied them the Cup Winners' Cup in a penalty decider. Who would they meet this time? A reunion with Benfica, who lead Parma 2–1 after a thrilling first-leg in Lisbon, is possible but the odds slightly favour Apsrilla, Brolin, Zola and company whose inconsistency is outweighed by a relish for the big occasion.

'Gunners on Course to Play the Game of European Patience.'
The Observer, Sunday 10 April, 1994. Patrick Barclay.

Alan Smith has been talking to Dan and me for more than an hour already but is still happy to talk about Arsenal further. Every time I interview a former player I use the clockwatching test as a gauge as to how things are going. Meaning, if the player being interviewed looks at his watch, or his eyes quickly scan a wall for a clock then it's invariably a sign to wind down the chat. I've been lucky that when this normally happens I have got all I need to file copy, but I must admit the longer an interview runs without this small and perfectly reasonable act taking place, the more I try and fit in as many questions as I can that were not on my original shorthand list.

One such question that crossed my mind was the crushing 3-1 home defeat in the European Cup against Benfica at Highbury in November 1991, which for me indelibly marked the end of George Graham's expressive title wining sides, hastening the second phase of his leadership in which we became a far cagier cup side. More than two decades on I ask Alan the questions that Paddy Barclay asked him in 1994 ahead of the decisive second-leg against Paris.

Did the shockwaves of losing to Benfica shape George Graham's – and the team's – attitude to European matches? Alan takes a sip of his coffee. Not to gain a second or two to think about his answer. No. I take the pause to mean that seismic defeat to the Eagles of Lisbon, which arguably shaped the next five years for Arsenal Football Club psyche, was so crushing. Even now nearly twenty-five years on the thought of it still frustrates.

After carefully placing his cup on the table, Alan looks me in the eye and says,

We had a very good team and squad in 1991. Although we weren't particularly favourites to win the European Cup in 91/92 we had such attacking options, which combined with a very commanding defence meant we could've been real contenders for the trophy had we beaten them.

I think I'm right in saying Benfica never scaled the heights of their performance against us against that season and did nothing in the cup after that. I think tactically he was very astute. When we got knocked out of the European Cup in 1991 by Benfica, by the time we got back into Europe for the 1993/94 European Cup Winners Cup run he made us harder to beat with 4-3-3 so learned from that.

Echoing what he'd told Paddy Barclay in 1994 he added to me,

I think after the 1–1 draw out in Lisbon maybe there was a certain notion that we had done the hard work and that if we played our normal game we would ease past Benfica at Highbury. I wouldn't say we underestimated them, they played well on the night, but there was a feeling we had been perhaps too naïve, or too open as we went searching for more goals.

I had scored four against Austria Vienna in the first round when we beat them 6–1 and we should have beaten Benfica too. Tony Adams had a chance close in and I had a chance to too. [With regret] We should've beaten them. They had the two Russian boys Isias and Yuran. [With a hint of a smile] They ended up at Millwall didn't they? That was a gutting night that was as we really should have won. I think it shaped George's thinking when we played in Europe after that defeat. And that feeling stayed with the boys who had lost to Benfica that night when we went to places like Torino and Paris, and subconsciously it must have made an impact in the home tie against PSG when it was so tight.

So you could argue that by losing to Benfica in 1991 it only made us more aware defensively by the time we played in Europe in 1993 and 1994, certainly against the likes of Torino, PSG and Palma whereby we were determined not to concede and everyone was keen to play their part to keep it that way.

Amy Lawrence recalled George's superb tactical nous in that tie, and in that run by relating to it his greatest night, by telling me,

I think when you get to a semi-final final you have to believe you are going to win. You have to believe you've got a chance in the last four of a knock-out competition otherwise you're mad. There was a momentum building. George Graham was very much into the tactical side of it all. The way tactically he managed the games up to that point, and the way he was able to point to the fact they outmanoeuvred an Italian team over two legs, meant the belief spread to the players and gave them a sense of trust.

A lot of those players had been there in Anfield 1989, admittedly a few years back but considering we are talking on the anniversary of that night [It's a quirk that I interview Amy on the 26th anniversary of that immortal night]. When I talk to the players of the class of 1989 who played on that night their reaction is a cross between thinking it's hilarious, to slightly awestruck, that George Graham read the script tactically, and in terms of how the scoring would go on the night.

Anfield 1989 was a good insight into George Graham, which would serve him so well five years later on that run, because tactically he was very strong. For example he played three at the back away at Manchester United in early April 1989 as a warm-up for the away game at Anfield that was the design to go to Anfield which was the big challenge, which was due to take place on 22 April before Hillsborough meant the game was pushed back until Friday 26 May.

Arsenal weren't as worried about Manchester United that season as they were about Liverpool, and George knew that game was coming up – earlier than it did of course. But he was that forward-thinking in his tactics he was already preparing to go to Anfield by trying out a revolutionary three at the back at Old Trafford, only weeks before the big one against title rivals Liverpool.

He put the ideas into play. The team talk he gave before Anfield in which he told the team to sit tight, don't go chasing for that first goal. You'd expect the opposite now of course in any Champions League game where they would be saying, 'You've got to score an early goal.' George was completely the opposite where he said calmly, 'Keep it tight. If you come in at 0-0 that's absolutely fine, that's exactly what we want, then get one early in the second-half, then they'll get nervous and we'll see if we can nick one before the end.'

You ask any of those players what they thought of George's tactics and instructions and they'll talk to you in a mixture of amusement and amazement. [I mention to Amy that's exactly the tone Alan Smith took and she smiles.] He called it. To relay it back to 93/94 the whole tactical side of George, was given even more credibility by going through after the two legs against Torino of Serie A.

My thoughts on Wrighty getting booked at Highbury in the second-leg of the semi-final against Paris were, 'Desperate. Desperate because it was Wrighty and everyone liked him. You could see what it meant to him. And desperate because he felt so critical to the Arsenal cause, and for him to lose in the final was a big blow. It was a huge concern to lose the greatest goal-scorer the club had ever seen at the time, and the immense determination with which he always played and realise he would not be playing in the final. And it was just a terrible thing for him not to play in the final because he deserved it. He didn't deserve to miss out.

Mike Francis, publisher and founding editor of *The Gooner* recalled with candour,

I honestly don't recall a great deal about the second-leg at Highbury Layth, but I'm sure it was one of those great European nights which sent shivers down your spine.

What turned out to be the winning goal came early from Kevin Campbell, possibly his greatest moment in an Arsenal shirt, allowing us to sing our new theme song for a large proportion of the ninety minutes plus injury time. The match seemed to last an age, far too long, because that's what happens when you're only one goal to the good and on the brink of a European final.

As a contributor to *The Gooner*, my editor Kevin Whitcher, recalls the night telling me, 'That second leg was a night of mixed emotions. A definite high with the achievement of making a first European final since 1980, but tinged with regret as Ian Wright received a yellow card that put him out of the final and left Gooners wondering if Arsenal could possibly beat their opponents Parma without their talismanic striker.'

As ever with Mike and Kevin they provide an insightful viewpoint because I hadn't really thought about the goal Kevin Campbell scored that night being arguably the most important goal he scored in his Arsenal career. A career which promised so much through his athleticism, sheer strength, power and pace.

How many of us still recall the goal he scored one-on-one against the sublime defensive artistry of Nottingham Forest's Des Walker. Walker was a ridiculously talented centre-half whose pace and positional awareness, not to mention technical ability and tactical awareness, made him one of England's best ever defenders in my opinion. Yet that night at Highbury in March 1990 (it's always the night games that stick in your memory) Campbell shrugged off Walker as if he wasn't there before powering a low shot to announce his arrival at the top level of English football.

Yet four years down the line Campbell had regressed alarmingly. I spoke to various former players about him over the last few years and they all said it was a shame the talent he showed in training was allowed to be overshadowed by an increasing lack of confidence. Once that vicious spiral starts, with an unconvinced crowd starting to look for your mistakes rather than support them and frustration spills over into derision and occasionally abuse then you know it's time to move on as a player.

Kevin Campbell in 1994 was on the cusp of that scenario. Which made his early goal against the Parisians even sweeter, for us of course, but also for him. Alan Smith, as ever, played exceptionally well with his back to goal, also playing a huge part in Campbell's vital goal in the eighth minute.

Picking up a throw from Lee Dixon on the right flank at a raucous Highbury where even the guys and girls in the east stand lower were making themselves heard, always a sign you were at a hugely important game at Arsenal Stadium, Smith gave the ball back to Arsenal's full back who then whipped in a head-height cross into the box. Campbell, in the middle, who had only started the match due to Paul Merson collecting an ankle injury in the last training session before the game met the ball powerfully and aimed it past a larger than expected gap between inconsistent goalkeeping showman Bernard Lama and his post.

Highbury erupted with joy, but I recall from there in the clock end that momentary ecstasy soon morphed into a nervousness which only worsened as the match progressed. As Tim Stillman, Arsenal season ticket holder and renowned *Arseblog* and *Goonersphere* columnist, tells me about that memorable night at Highbury,

The Paris Saint Germain semi-final at Highbury really sticks in my mind because it was my first-ever midweek game at Highbury. I became a season ticket holder in 1992, at the age of eight, but midweek games were strictly off the menu in my first two seasons. I'd watched much of the run to the League Cup Final in 1993 via video recorded ITV highlights. For the Cup Winners Cup in 1993/94 the gruff voice of Brian Moore was the medium through which I digested Arsenal's run.

Having watched the destruction of Standard Liège on television, I tried to convince my mum to let me go to the quarter-final against Torino to no avail. The tension of that second-leg triumph at Highbury caused me to redouble my efforts for the visit of PSG in the semi-final and eventually, after much nagging, mum relented.

PSG were a fantastic side stocked with world-class talent. That summer at USA 1994, I'd begin to become more conversant with continental stars, but the likes of Valdo, Raí, Weah and Ginola might as well have come from another planet.

I remember the elation of Kevin Campbell's goal and then the good hours' worth of tension and nausea following. The moment that really sticks in my mind is Seaman making a right hash of his attempt to bowl the ball out to Winterburn, which ended in him tossing the ball at the feet of the mercurial Valdo just 25 yards from goal.

Fortunately Arsenal were able to smother him in time. Then there was Wright's yellow card which momentarily sucked the vigour from the crowd. It's probably a trick of memory, but I'm sure supporters began whistling at the referee well before stoppage time. Those last five minutes were unbearable but the explosion of relief and joy at the final whistle has stayed with me ever since.

Acclaimed Arsenal author Jon Spurling added of that evening,

The semi-final return against PSG – what a night! There was the drama of Ian
Wright being booked and therefore ruling himself out of the Final but in a game of
such fines margins, Arsenal squeezed and squeezed PSG, and David Ginola, not for
the first time, was relentlessly pursued by Lee Dixon.

I celebrated Kevin Campbell's winning goal like a crazy man. Even early on
I sensed that chances would be few and far between. Of course, on a weekly basis,
playing in that style was never going to win us the league but George made the best
of what he had, and that was apparent in the final against a far more gifted Parma
side.

This was George's last hurrah, and if you think about it, Paul Davis had only
just returned, Anders Limpar had been frozen out, and Paul Merson was misfiring
all over the place. The team was shorn of skill. The Cup Winners' Cup run was
bottom line: do-or-die football. No gloss, no finesse really, just an ethos of 'do the
job.' And we did just that. Anyone who's read my books and articles knows I'm a
huge admirer of George Graham. On the big occasion, when it absolutely mattered,
he was a master tactician whose sides were never outfought or outwitted, and they
could go toe to toe with anyone.

If any player personified that era it was probably Alan Smith an underrated player
who always did the business when it absolutely mattered. Anfield 1989, Parma
1994, and a massive thorn in Liverpool, United's and Tottenham's sides. A big game
player, and I'm thrilled it was him who scored the winner in Copenhagen. I look
back on those Highbury nights against Torino and PSG with as much affection as
anything under Wenger.

Fellow Arsenal author Dave Seager explained, 'I clearly recall we were underdogs
against PSG who went on to win the French League by a huge margin. We'd
drawn in Paris and at Highbury Super Kevin Campbell nodded home a Dixon
cross early on and we again held out singing 'One-Nil-To-The-Arsenal' over and
over again.'

Darren Epstein also recalled that immortal Highbury evening,

Kevin Campbell scored right at the start. He was immense. Kevin got a lot of stick
from the fans, his first touch wasn't great, but I always felt he was unduly criticised.
He had some immense games, Benfica and PSG especially. Truthfully he was a
handful for European teams, he bullied them. The home game was so tense, it really
was on a knife edge, and the Wright booking.

Fleet Street journalist Steve Tongue who covered Arsenal's European Cup
Winners' Cup run that season told me,

Paris St Germain was an exciting semi-final draw as they were just emerging as a force and they had knocked out Real Madrid and had talents like Ginola and Weah. I suspect Arsenal were a bit worried about them but were on such a good run in the Premier League that they felt they could shut anyone out. So a 1-1 was another good away result and I think PSG were shocked at Highbury by Arsenal's sheer physicality and tempo, shutting down their creative players.

The programme that night, already a collector's item, contained this gem from Jonathan Pearce, (then Capital Gold sports editor) who wrote,

Two weeks ago Arsenal probably surprised PSG with their attacking game. The team turned in an excellent all-round performance and were unlucky not to come back to Highbury with a lead.

Frank McLintock, the last Arsenal skipper to lift a European trophy, and who's in our Capital Gold commentary team again tonight, is confident the Gunners will go through. He's banking on a 1-0 win.

Perhaps George Graham's pre-match programme notes summed the night up best with his uncanny prescience ahead of big games – not to mention providing a spine-tingling rallying cry to anyone who cared about The Arsenal.

A quick read through is enough to evoke memories of those great and much-missed Highbury nights. The intensity catches me off guard and George's passion somehow makes my throat catch with emotion. God how I love The Arsenal. [With thanks to Steve Tongue for providing me with a copy after I couldn't locate mine.]

On nights like this, managers often say 'we're treating this as just another game.' I won't. This is the pinnacle of our season so far. Tonight could prove a huge landmark in the history of our club. I played in the Arsenal team that won the Fairs Cup in 1970. That's the only European trophy Arsenal has won. That's not enough for a club of our stature.

Everyone in the dressing room knows how much Europe matters to our supporters. It matters even more to us. The club's history is all about winning trophies. It's all or nothing tonight. We respond to that sort of challenge. The players deserve great credit for the way they've adapted to European football. There's a huge gap between our often frantic game and the patience needed to succeed in European competitions.

They were very mature in both games against Torino, and in the Parc de Princes. I've read stories this week that the risk of a second yellow card will inhibit some of our player tonight. I don't think so. When you're out on the pitch, you only think about winning. The thought of the will fill their minds, not cards from the referee. We couldn't have asked for harder opponents. Paris St Germain are one of the most talented teams in France. They boast a dozen or so internationals, including George Weah, David Ginola and three Brazilian stars.

If we can knock them out, that will show our calibre.

It certainly did George, it certainly did.

9

Arsenal vs Parma (n): It's Quite True!

The European Cup Winners' Cup Final. Arsenal 1 Parma 0. (Arsenal win the 1994 European Cup Winners' Cup.) 4 May 1994.

Life itself is the most wonderful fairy tale.

Hans Christian Andersen.

The first week of May 1994 was a momentous time. More than 20,000 Arsenal fans geared themselves up to reach Copenhagen by train, plane and automobiles the world was slowly digesting the dreadful news that the legendary racing driver Ayrton Senna had died during a race on Sunday 1 May 1994. The ferociously talented Senna, who had won three Formula One world championships, was killed in an accident while leading the San Marino Grand Prix leaving the world shocked. Prince may have been Number One that week in the UK with 'The Most Beautiful Girl in the World', but for Mike Francis, publisher and founding editor of *Gooner* he only had eyes for his partner Sharon, and The Arsenal of course.

Mike takes up the story:

After seeing off Paris Saint Germain in the semi-finals it was on to the final then and the mad scramble for tickets and travel. However, I don't actually recall it being too difficult to get a ticket because I also managed to get one for my Arsenal supporting other half, Sharon. Not that she was too sure about going because she'd never flown before and was nervous about the prospect to say the least.

We'd decided to turn the trip into a short break and flew to the Danish capital on the Sunday prior to the game. Sharon always took great pleasure in reminding me that I was so concerned about her being okay to fly that I ended up looking more nervous than her when we boarded the plane to such an extent that a flight attendant asked me if I was alright!

A very vivid memory of our first few hours in Copenhagen was turning on the TV in the hotel and watching a local channel showing a clip of a car crashing at the Formula 1 Grand Prix from Italy. The commentary wasn't in English so it took a while before it dawned on us that the reason the clip was being shown repeatedly was because the consequences were fatal and the driver was Ayrton Senna, one of the greatest racing drivers of all-time. Unsurprisingly it was a story which was to dominate the news for much of the time we were in Denmark.

We spent our first couple of days familiarising ourselves with the city and doing the typical touristy stuff. We visited the Little Mermaid, the Rundetaarn (Round Tower) and Tivoli Gardens where I was photographed with a cannon. Surely a good omen. By Tuesday evening large numbers of Arsenal and Parma fans had started arriving in the city for the game the following evening. In contrast to the scenes we would experience when we returned to Copenhagen in 2000, there was a great atmosphere with rival supporters drinking together and swapping scarves and stories.

The pubs were doing a roaring trade in the local brew, which to most English fans amazement was not Carlsberg, but Tuborg. There were also significant volumes drunk of a strong Danish beer called Faxe in honour of our Danish international John Jensen whose nickname it was due, apparently, to being rather partial to it. Unfortunately, Jensen was injured for the final in his home country.

Mike, who I am pleased to say now counts as a friend after kindly allowing me to contribute to *The Gooner* over the last few years, also made a very interesting point about what it was like to be an Arsenal fan, not only in that improbable week but long before the instant age of social media where everyone can voice an opinion on twitter.

One of Arsenal's biggest and most influential fans said to me,

We were clearly the underdogs as our Italian opponents, Parma, had dazzling array of attacking talent at their disposal with Zola, Asprilla and Brolin expected to cause us plenty of problems. Our goal-scoring talisman Ian Wright was suspended which was almost undoubtedly a consequence of appearing on the front cover of the latest *Gooner* which came out on the night he picked up the fateful yellow card in the semi-final second-leg. However, despite all this, I don't remember being nervous or pessimistic on the day of the game. Perhaps that was just a sign of the times because with no platform to bemoan our misfortune, champion the opposition or berate our own players and manager, the fire of negativity was not fuelled and people were more likely to be swayed by the feel-good factor of being in a final.

I would compare and contrast that view with the internet age where fans seem to enjoy wallowing in a sense of despair and self-pity. I digress, but I do think it was still possible in 1994 to enjoy an occasion without the predicted outcome being the only criteria on which your enjoyment could be measured.

Another person who was enjoying the lead up to the final was the illustrious sportswriter Patrick Barclay who told me,

Early May 1994 was an incredible time in news as well as sport with the death of Ayrton Senna. But if we're talking solely about Arsenal at that time I was intrigued by their run. I had been covering their European progress for the *Observer* and was particularly interested in their solid defence. I remember writing a piece about Tony Adams on the Sunday.

I'm sure even diehard Gunners fans like yourself Layth, who having followed them all across Europe on that run would be the first to admit Arsenal were not a great team but what they did have was a great defence. And I tried to convey a sense of how important Tony Adams was for them. For me Tony Adams was the original thou shalt not pass centre-back. How much would he be worth in today's market? Feel free to use the article if you can find it.

Never have I acted so quickly on a comment thankfully finding his piece during my research in the astonishing British Library:

The phrase 'a born leader' is somewhat hackneyed but in the case of Tony Adams it is quite possible to imagine that, upon being released from the umbilical cord, he organised the nurses in a line and then claimed offside against the midwife.

Actually the first fourteen years of his life are not chronicled, although we do know that Adams came to Highbury an instinctive commander. 'As soon as I saw him play,' says Don Howe, 'I was sure he'd be a captain of the Arsenal. I gave him his debut at seventeen and, when George Graham took over as manager I knew he'd got another Frank McLintock on his hands.

The comparison is irresistible. McLintock, though not quite a great player was a great captain, a double winner. Adams had already led the club to two championships and, last season, a cup double, and, on Wednesday in Copenhagen, he hopes to become only the second Arsenal captain after McLintock to lift a European trophy. Yet the suspicion remains that Europe might prove his achilles' heel, even if all the arrows shot by Paris in the semi-final failed to hurt him. Adams, thus far, has done the most to confound those who felt that a defence built to withstand the bufferings of the English game might be circumnavigated, as when Benfica visited Highbury in 1991, by more nimble overseas craft. Only one goal has been conceded in the last six matches of the Cup Winners' Cup campaign and now comes the ultimate challenge: Parma. A consciously stylish team whose attack features not only two ball players of the sort Arsenal are supposed to fear, Gianfranco Zola and Tomas Brolin, but the orthodox, bewildering speed merchant Faustino Asprilla.

They would have loved taking on the Adams of a few years ago. Now even his habitual detractors are not so sure. Having suffered for his precociousness – most memorably when, fourteen months after a fine England debut in Spain [England won 4–2] tempted Bobby Robson to let him be dubbed a new Bobby Moore. He was turned by Marco van Basten into something more closely resembling a rag doll, he has thrived through resilience, diligence and experience. It takes an exceptional central defender to reach maturity when young. Moore was an example. Being mentioned in the same breath as him did Adams no favours. For all his natural strength and equally natural leadership, one mortal head could not possibly carry all he knew.

As an Essex boy he grew up supporting West Ham and came to Highbury with an obvious taste for knocking the ball about. The Arsenal academy, grooming a generation of Adams, Michael Thomas, David Rocastle et al who were to become champions, quickly pointed out his limitations in this regard as he emerged as the symbol of George Graham's creation, in which a higher priority was placed on discomfort with losing than comfort on the ball. During last spring's cup exploits Graham said, 'He's been a hero of mine for years.' A hero of the crowd too.

'Highbury Lion Dropping Dead the Donkey Tag'. Sunday 1 May 1994.
Patrick Barclay, Sports Journalist of the Year 1994.

The interview with Alan Smith has gone well. As Patrick Barclay said to me in his fulsome praise of the player 'he is a very impressive character'. One of the things I immediately liked about Alan as a person was the fact there was no hyperbole. What he said was honest and considered. If he told you something it was because it was the truth. As we talked I got the feeling the latter part of his career didn't go as well as he would have liked, certainly compared to the glories of the earlier segment of his time with the Gunners. And yet as he contemplated football without the club, that he would be indelibly linked with, he also achieved what, for many, was his crowning glory: hitting a brilliant winner in the final of a European trophy. Intrigued at this all-too-evident dichotomy I ask him how he summed up the latter part of his time at Arsenal. With feeling and complete honesty he answers,

The last couple of years of my Arsenal career weren't happy ones for me. I had always been among the goals but, towards the end, the goals were going in around me. I did actually put in a transfer request right at the end of my career at Highbury because I simply wasn't happy, but George wouldn't let me go.

Yet with hindsight, I'd have to say I was glad I stayed at the club as I wouldn't have had the European Cup Winners Cup run of 1994. And also because I'm closely associated with Arsenal now, and I would have got injured if I'd had gone anywhere else for a year or two and would have had to call it a day anyway, so yes I am very pleased to have stayed and been a part of such a victory.

I also got the sense that having played in very good teams, staffed with powerful but creative players, the later years at Arsenal didn't produce or accumulate such technically proficient or mentally tough enough footballers. His answer was as revealing as it was true, as every Arsenal fan who watched them around that time can testify.

Those years towards the end were a bit of a grind. We were signing players who weren't generally good enough for the shirt, not good enough to play for The Arsenal certainly, compared to the league title winning sides. So it was a bit disappointing.

When you've had a great midfield it's harder to play without one. When I joined, Paul Davis and Steve Williams were part of the Arsenal midfield, two quality players. So towards the end I kept thinking what's going here? We became a bit of a cup team and if Wrighty didn't score we didn't score. We also didn't have too much width to our game either. My confidence took a nosedive and I was missing chances left right and centre I would have normally snapped up just a year or two before.

I was there to score and if I wasn't scoring my confidence took a nosedive. I remember at the start of the 1991 season I didn't score for the first nine or ten games. I went to the gaffer and he said, 'Don't worry you're still doing the right things, the goals will come, just keep going'. So I did, and I scored against Southampton and then I went and scored in about eight or nine consecutive matches after that. But if you're not scoring you do tend to snatch at things. You always want to go on until your mid-thirties not least because the lads who were playing then started earning big money! [Laughs] When Wenger came in he bumped up all the boys' wages to be near to people like Bergkamp, which was credit to Wenger. But I don't have too many regrets about the game. I had thirteen very good years in the game. The average career of a footballer is seven years. I was fortunate. You do have to make the most of it.

I loved the way he was so matter-of-fact about everything. Whether it be playing in good, bad or indifferent teams, winning or not winning trophies, maybe that's what professional footballers have to do to keep balanced.

He adds, 'It is about timing. Look at Gary Lineker. He's won an FA Cup and a Spanish Cup. Alan Shearer. OK he won a title at Blackburn – but not much else. Sometimes it is just about timing and good luck.' My dictaphone whirrs away, but for good measure I still take shorthand notes. As we have talked for the best part of two hours our time with this modest, self-effacing man, who also happens to be an Arsenal legend, and one that the esteemed Patrick Barclay no less would have in his All Time Arsenal XI, is coming to an end.

I ask him quickly, 'What would you say was your favourite ever Arsenal goal?'

It would be the header at Anfield because it was so important. It didn't look much but me, Bouldy and Tony would always line-up and quite often Tony would peel round the back in training and we'd always say to George 'why the bloody hell are we always doing this, it never works on a match-day?'

The Cup Winners Cup Winner was great – one of the best goals of my career. The one I got against Norwich in May 1989 in a 5–0 win was good. When John Lukic just launched it and it came to me and I just hit it as cleanly as I could and it went it. The one against Liverpool in a 3–0 win in Dec 1990 was a good one as well. I hit that with a bit of dip and it just went under Grobellar's body.

Between 1992 and 1994 the back four and Wrighty were our main strengths, but from 1987 to 1992 we had very good players and were very disciplined. We worked very hard too. In training we would always work very hard in closing down from the front. Merse or whoever would show them inside and we would do certain practice sessions where that was all we would work on sometimes. It was driven into us.

We'd do a bit of shooting practice at the end but that was it. But I enjoyed it. I never got bored. It was all short sharp stuff. Rival managers used to say, 'No-one works as hard as Arsenal in closing down from the front'. George would always cite the example of Ian Rush of how hard centre-forwards should work, the way they should sprint across the full backs. I did work that hard.

We had a great togetherness, we had a great team spirit. There were no cliques at the club. We had a real fighting spirit. You couldn't bully us. We were all in it together. We'd all stick together. We'd all go out together. I'd dip in and out of the Tuesday club. I wasn't one of the founders! Merse and Tony were!

We also used to go to Spain for end of season trips to Porto Banus. We'd always stick together. I remember one time we all got on stage and started singing, 'George, George, stand by me', and George actually walked into this bar! [We all laugh]. He turned round and walked straight out again. He would always pride himself on finding somewhere nice the lads didn't know about!

Time is running out. I think simple questions again. Who was the best attacking player you ever played with?

[Without hesitation] Paul Merson, because he was such a selfless player. He could really pick a pass. If you were in a better position he would look up and find you. We had a good rapport. The best finisher was undoubtedly Wrighty. He was such a difficult player to play against because he was such an individual. I never really developed an understanding with him. But Merse was my favourite player to play with, and he was superb during that Cup Winners' Cup run.

Which culminated in wonderful Copenhagen, with The Miracle of Copenhagen.

10

The Miracle of Copenhagen

The whole world is a series of miracles.

Hans Christian Andersen.

The travelling support that night was one of the best I can ever remember.

Alan Smith in conversation with Dan McCarthy and the author, 2015.

Parma are a great team of individuals, but the greater the odds against us, the better we seem to perform.

George Graham, before the game.

Alan Smith tells me,

When you get to the final you think you may have a chance. But with Wrighty suspended, and with us having a lot of injuries, and they had some fantastic players. The midfield we had that night was never a first team starting eleven, certainly not a first choice midfield starting eleven. I remember we had Ian Selly, Paul Davis, Stevie Morrow in midfield that day lined up in a 4-3-3.

When we were in the tunnel looking over at Asprilla, Brolin, Zola, Buffon the Italian team looked immaculate, and when they strode out looking the dogs bollocks, well ... you just look at each other, look at your Arsenal teammates, your Arsenal mates and you think we are second favourites. But with football, and with Arsenal's history just because you're second favourites it doesn't mean you're going to lose. Look at Anfield 1989.

They had a very good team at the time – half of Italy's World Cup squad who went to America that year. I remember the night before the final: We were training on the Parken pitch. We were first on. And when we came off Parma were waiting on the side-line waiting for us to come off so they could go on and train, we said at the time they looked at us like we were a piece of shit, I couldn't tell you who said it but it was a great way to wind ourselves up!

The crowd spurred us on that night. The travelling Arsenal support was one of the best I can ever remember. When we went out to warm up before the game, I was with Tony Adams, and I remember saying, 'Bloody Hell Tone we've got some support behind tonight!' And if you remember, the Parken was a bit like Highbury with the stands right on top of you, almost encroaching on the pitch. The Parken was almost like a home from home, not least with 30,000 Gooners in the crowd but also the way it was designed, with stands that sort of looked familiar in shape and design, so we felt at home. And of course, they were red and white Arsenal flags everywhere so it very much felt like a home game. That was really important to us as a team. We felt very encouraged by that atmosphere, and knowing so many Arsenal fans had travelled to support their team.

I ask him a question only someone without experience of playing professional football would ask. I say what went through your mind when you were just about to shoot? Alan looks at me like I'm mad, 'Nothing. Nothing went through my mind when I was just about to shoot'. I persist in wanting to know about that moment, that glorious moment. But what made you take the shot I say?

Well, it was there to be hit. There were two lads either side of me converging on me so I had to hit it. It was there to be hit. I didn't score many from outside the box – but I scored a few. It was just one of those where there was nothing else on, so when I chested it down and it bounced up nicely I thought it was worth a crack so I just hit it.

Again, those simple questions. What did you think after it went in I ask?

I couldn't see the ball. It started off as I say when the two lads converged on me, and then the keeper kind of dived in front of hit so he blocked my vision in seeing the ball after I hit it, so the first time I actually saw it was when it hit the post and went in. So I just thought, 'Oh yeah, it's in – thank god for that!' My teammates didn't say much to me when we were celebrating. They were just jumping on me and celebrating and shouting. But we all knew it was early doors in the game so we couldn't get too carried away as there was still a long way to go.

As someone who was at the Parken (behind the opposite goal to where Alan achieved sporting immortality) I felt an immediate release of pent up relief made manifest in the longest, loudest guttural yell. He smiles as I ask him how he felt at the final whistle,

Ecstatic, obviously. It was a fantastic result. Dave Seaman had to do a lot of great saves on the night. He actually had to have an injection in his ribs at half-time during the game because he was in such pain. We hardly had another chance during the rest of the game. My job was to hold it up just to take the heat off our defenders, and

I think I did that really. But in terms of us getting the ball in the box, we didn't do that much at all, so when the final whistle went, yeah it was fantastic.

Arsenal Football Club hasn't won too many European trophies, the Fairs Cup in 1969/70 and Copenhagen 1994, so when the final whistle went and we realised we had won, well, it was fantastic.

I mention the fact my pals and I, and about 20,000 other Gooners, celebrated long and hard into the night. But I'm always intrigued to hear what the players did on their night of victory.

(As an aside I tell him when I asked Ray Parlour that about the party the night The Invincibles won the league at White Hart Lane he told me with a ready laugh, 'I don't know, I was out celebrating for three days!') 'What did we do that night?' Alan ponders:

We flew home. We flew home because George Graham said we had to! The reason was because if we hadn't have won in Copenhagen we would have needed to win or get something at the weekend at St James's Park against Newcastle United which was the last day of the season, to guarantee European football for the next season. That was how driven George was. So we couldn't we plan on stopping there and having a party. We just had some champagne on the flight home. I wouldn't say it was an anti-climax as such because you can never say winning a European trophy was an anti-climax, but in terms of the celebrations, well we heard about all those thousands of Arsenal fans having such a great night. About them all having a party until the early hours, or in many cases until the next day, and we wished we could have joined in the party! I've talked to some fans who say they had the best ever celebrations in Copenhagen that night so it would have been nice to have joined them. During the lap of honour I don't think I've ever seen so many grown men cry, that and Anfield 1989!

We just flew back to Stanstead about four or five in the morning. And went home. [Laughs] Although I can confirm we did sing 'One-Nil-to-the-Arsenal' after the game quite a few times! There were some press at Stanstead when got back, so we had our pictures taken with the trophy again. But what do you do at five in the morning at Stanstead Airport?!

Dan, my friend, says 'apparently Johnny Jensen stayed and had a party in a bar in Copenhagen until the early hours?' Alan replies dryly as ever, 'Well, it was alright for him, wasn't it, he was out injured ...'

Patrick Barclay talks of that team and that wonderful night in Copenhagen. He tells me,

From 1991 the attacking force was nowhere near the same as it was prior to then. Nevertheless what the Arsenal team of that era did have, that season in Europe in particular, was an absolute wealth of striking options and goal-scorers. So for that reason although we may think of Alan Smith's winner against Parma as the peak of his goal-scoring career it wasn't because he was almost marginal in the side by then and only started the final in Copenhagen because first choice striker Ian Wright was suspended. In a way, as much as his contribution to the great Arsenal teams of 1989 and 1991 was possibly slightly understated under George Graham I think it's worth remembering that for all the people who talk about Ian Wright being one of the great goal-scorers of Arsenal's history, the fact that Alan Smith was the leading scorer in two championship winning campaigns as well as being the only goal-scorer on the night the club won their second European trophy in Copenhagen I think marks him out as a really great contributor to the George Graham era.

I reported on the game in Copenhagen but I was with the *Observer* so I wouldn't have had it in the paper until the Sunday after the match. For the final I can remember thinking absolutely Arsenal were not the favourites. As I recall Parma were the holders of the trophy, and they had all their best players, all their top players on show.

Brolin, Asprilla, Zola were their crack players then. It's interesting because we talk about the trip of top players at Real Madrid and at Barcelona but they were the top trio of that time in European football no doubt. Three really outstanding players. Asprilla's pace was astonishing. He played right at the front with Zola, and Brolin just off him. It was a formidable attack.

In the early stages of the game it seemed to be going to expectations and I remember Steve Bould making a great tackle in the opening minutes as Asprilla threatened to cut through the Arsenal defence like a knife. I think Brolin hit the post, as Arsenal struggled to hold on.

Patrick, originally perceptive as ever and as the author of that rare beast, a best-selling and critically acclaimed book said with the knowledge of a man steeped in football, football writing, and football history, 'I often described Arsenal at that time as a 'heart-breaking side', meaning they were a side that broke the hearts of the opposition, very much in the Herbert Chapman mould of that great Arsenal team of the 1930s.

After Parma had gone through their repertoire of attacking brilliance, Arsenal simply whacked the ball in the net to go one nil up. Ok, there was a defensive mistake but it was a magnificent left-foot shot from the vastly underrated Alan Smith which went in off the goalkeepers near post in a wonderfully clean strike, and that just turned the game. I just think there was a feeling Arsenal would do enough to get through. It wasn't the best performance but defensively it was very strong. What a performance it was to beat such performers in Parma. In a way it was almost a forgotten triumph or a half-triumph, or a barely remembered triumph on a national scale at least, of course it wasn't seen like that by Arsenal fans as it will obviously be remembered by them with such fond memories. But I think it has been also forgotten by people about what a good team Parma were. The fact that has been lost is another indication of the fact that the Gunners win that season is a forgotten triumph even if it was, as you say Layth, The Miracle of Copenhagen.

I think when people look back on that season in European terms the first thing they remember is the 1994 European Cup Final in Athens between AC Milan and Barcelona, with Fabio Cappelo's Milan for me giving the greatest performance ever in European Cup final or Champions League European Cup final. And they don't remember too much about the other finals that year. For example tell me off the top of your head who won the UEFA Cup Final that year?

I desperately try and remember, pulling Milan's city rivals Inter from a brain packed with useless sporting information and not much else. Half-recalling the fact they beat Austrian's Salzburg in the final play, in one of those unfair quirks UEFA seems to enjoy, in Vienna. Patrick says,

Exactly. It was hard to recall. Which would be the same to non-Arsenal fans. Which is a shame as they deserved huge credit for their results and defensive performances that season. The view in the press box before the final was that we were to watch an Arsenal team past its best and we fully expected them to lose. But, during the game, what I recollect is that the atmosphere was superb. I think of the magnificent noise those travelling Arsenal fans made during the whole game, and it also has to be remembered they far outnumbered their Parma counterparts in a huge show of loyalty in making the trip to Denmark's capital.

They were certainly the more vociferous and made for a real rollicking atmosphere, they were very good. I remember being in the streets of Copenhagen before the game, and don't forget this was less than a decade since Heysel when all English clubs had been rightly banished from Europe after that, so we'd grown accustomed to being a little ashamed and nervous of travelling fans. But I remember thinking that Arsenal fans were a credit to English supporters abroad. So the atmosphere on the day in Copenhagen was very good and much more light hearted than we'd become accustomed to after the terrible tragedies in the decade previously. During the match there was a tremendous atmosphere generated by the Arsenal fans in the ground. I have really fond memories of it. The general atmosphere in and around the game was kind of refreshing and reassuring after the shame we all felt from 1985, and still do.

I ask then ask Patrick whether he thought the win against Parma was the 'Miracle of Copenhagen'. He thinks for a while and then answers as studiously and insightfully as ever,

It was a European trophy Arsenal won that night, and it provided in the end The Miracle of Copenhagen. I think it was very miraculous because what it did was provide a huge splash of colour in that season. It was an occasion and contained moments of heroism including from Alan Smith, who if you wished anybody to round off their career with a flourish it would be Alan Smith. He was an exemplary footballer. Even in his behaviour. He was one of those players who when someone says 'to have a successful team or to be a good player you have to have a nasty streak in you', you would simply dangle his name in front of them and say 'well, no you don't'. He was the man who led the Arsenal front line to two championships on the home front, and a European trophy on the away front, and it was all done without going in the book. He had a great attitude, but was also a terrific player who scored goals when you needed him to. And yet in that season I think that goal in Copenhagen was only his seventh of the campaign because what he said as soon as Ian Wright came to the club was 'right, okay, I now see my role as chipping in with my fair share of goals but mainly making goals for him'. I think if you look at the players Alan Smith played alongside, such as Gary Lineker at Leicester City, Ian Wright and Paul Merson at Arsenal, they all made reputations even if Merson didn't quite fulfil every last bit of his potential, but he got pretty good figures [423 matches, ninety-nine goals for The Arsenal]. And that ain't by chance, that was because they played alongside Alan Smith.

I would sum up his career by calling him an Arsenal great. I really would. He was a little unlucky not to earn more England caps but he was firmly an Arsenal great. What I also liked about him was that he was wonderful from the point of his of his unselfishness because he was the absolute dedicated team player. It may sound slightly strange but when I think of Alan Smith I think of Wayne Rooney, in terms of his unselfishness for the cause. When people talk about Rooney at times they say he should be more selfish and so on but I say to that, 'You don't have to be more selfish to score lots of goals'.

For me the guy who plays for the team as well as himself is doubly valuable. Look at Marco van Basten. I saw on play on many occasion as he wasn't what you would call a selfish player was he? He was a team player. Wayne Rooney is a team player. Alan Smith was a team player. Alan Smith is the player I think of when I think of an absolute team player as a forward. I would say categorically he was the football young players and young people should aspire to be. I really would. I would say his attitude to the game was fantastic, absolutely first rate, although it's probably too late now as most kids would think he was simply a Sky or BBC commentator! But for me he was really an outstanding player, most probably because of his self-effacing attitude, which was very different from say, Wrighty in that respect.

If I had to write a best ever Arsenal team sheet for me Alan Smith would be on it. It would be Wrighty, Bergkamp, Henry and Alan Smith somewhere in the formation, it would be very hard to leave him out.

I listen in awe of this great journalist and broadcaster, a man who has forgotten more about football than I will ever know, a man utterly respected by his peers in a tough industry that I am still learning my trade in, a man who was been generous to a fault with his time and I think if he is saying Alan Smith should be in Arsenal's best ever starting eleven then that's good enough for me. I also think how fortunate I am to have interviewed both men, hugely impressive in their fields, for the book.

Emboldened I mention a theory that has been taking shape during all the many interviews, conversations, writing and research I have undertaken throughout the course of the book. It's now or ever to suggest it to a true journalist legend.

I say to Patrick, breathlessly, 'I've got this theory.' He silent nods sagely indicating for me to continue.

If Arsenal hadn't won the 1994 European Cup Winners' Cup Final they wouldn't have had the prospect of European football the year after to look forward to which was, as many have said, a huge, unusual event back then which was then a major distraction through the traumatic 1994/95 season. The team, certainly the defence, would have been broken up far earlier which would have meant that when Arsene Wenger took over in September 1996 he may not have had the famed defensive line to rely on, and the amazing subsequent success he enjoyed, certainly in the first part of his reign, the Highbury Years, would never have happened.

Whether the fact that there would have been far more focus on an ageing back four through the ructions of the 1994/95 season and then under Bruce Rioch. If we didn't have the 1994/95 Cup Winners' Cup to look forward to as a distraction during those momentous, fractured last months under George Graham, and in a sense that further European run of 1994/95 took the focus off an underachieving and ageing team domestically that would have been ripe for an overhaul had there not been that European run gained by The Miracle of Copenhagen. As well as so many other off-field distractions, meaning that when Wenger took over from Bruce Rich he could have had a very different back four, and the success we had under him may not have been achieved as our defence which was the cornerstone of those trophy laden years could have looked so very different. To put it simply, winning in 1994 changed the course of Arsenal history allowing Wenger the option of still having the back four in place during two tumultuous years off the pitch at Arsenal between May 1994 and September 1996?

Patrick takes his time and thinks deeply, as I wonder whether this man I hugely respect will think I am a complete idiot, before replying 'I agree with that'. Carefully choosing every word he continues,

I watched the highlights of the Parma game the other day I was struck by the resilience of the defence. Even in the opening minutes that tackle by Bould on Asprilla, which was a statement of intent, you don't get tackling like that anymore. It really was extraordinary. If Steve Bould was in the game now goodness knows what his value would be. Bearing in mind he was always in Tony Adams shadow, so I think yes Layth, the result in Copenhagen – The Miracle of Copenhagen – means you can definitely sustain the theory that that result in May 1994 actually helped produce a good start to the Wenger era just over two years later and look what happened then. Because winning in 1994 vindicated the retention of the back five, I always say back five as I always include the goalkeeper David Seaman in that combination. So yes I think you may well be right in the original theory you are propounding.

Overjoyed that the doyen of journalism has just agreed with a theory of mine the interview comes to a close. I mention to Patrick that the pies are on me at Piebury Corner next time he covers and Arsenal game and he laughs and says that sounds like a good idea, you're on. 'I'll tell you what you can give me in return Layth: some of your energy for journalism and writing, football and Arsenal in particular, it's infectious and incredible. I love it.' Stunned, I thank him profusely like the gibbering idiot I normally am and we part agreeing to catch up again soon.

Interview over. When I get home that evening, after I put my three Junior Gunners to bed, I pour myself a large glass and an involuntary smile appears across my face. 'What are you smiling about?' my long suffering partner Claire asks, more out of curiosity, that I'm up to something. I look at her, with a widening grin, 'Oh, nothing,' I reply.

Amy Lawrence recalls that amazing week brilliantly encapsulating the sense of anticipation, wonder, excitement and disbelief explaining,

For the final, without going into too much detail, we played West Ham United on the Saturday before at Highbury. In those days in order to get cheap flights anywhere in Europe you had to stay over on the Saturday night. So our little gang of mates had booked up to go to Copenhagen on the Saturday, meaning we had to leave the West Ham game before the end. It was 0–0 when we left so it was probably quite fortunate as we ended up losing 2–0. [Laughs]

It was quite a strange situation. One of our mates lived nearby and we had left all our bags at his house and we just all trooped out of Highbury to collect our gear and walk down Arsenal tube station while the game was still going on! We stayed with some friends of friends in Copenhagen so we were there for a few days beforehand which was great.

There was a fantastic sense of build-up and the atmosphere in Copenhagen was incredibly special and you got the feeling that 99 per cent of Danes wanted Arsenal to win. Going back to the Scandinavian history of providing lots of supporters of Arsenal and I think the fact that English football was generally more popular than Italian football in that part of the world, in that region of Europe. So we were really welcomed. There was a lot of warmth and a lot of fun, you could describe it as a four day party in Copenhagen really. By the time the final came around there were people who barely made it to the ground!

We were not far from the main square where the majority of Arsenal fans had gathered hours before the match. We spent a lot of time at a bar called Keegans, I'm not sure why but it was our local in Copenhagen. We were right behind the goal. The whole experience being at the Parken was fantastic. It felt out of this world to be there watching Arsenal in a European final. It was one of those games where you sat at the stadium pinching yourself that you were there. There were so many Arsenal fans in the stadium. There was a real consciousness on the night that Arsenal fans outnumbered Parma fans by a quite staggering degree, something like nine or ten to one. Also there was no hint of trouble between the two sets of supporters inside the ground or around the town before or after the game in a direct contrast to what was to follow back in Copenhagen when Arsenal next played there in 2000. It was all quite friendly and people were very, very excited.

What I do remember is that the Parma fans all seemed to be very well dressed. [We both laugh at the memory]. Certainly compared to the Arsenal fans! They all seemed to have nice ironed slacks and smart V-neck jumpers wrapped casually around their cool shirts, and loafers. I remember it was a real contrast to the slightly dishevelled, drunken, slightly worn Arsenal supporters who weren't as sophisticated as the Italians! We were all looking at them thinking 'they're quite different', but I'm sure they were thinking the same thing about the thousands of Gooners who had descended on Copenhagen.

The atmosphere and drama at the game itself was brilliant, a mix between nervy and brilliant as we all screamed for the final whistle. It was definitely one of those games which stops you in your tracks, the fact you are at a European final. Little things like seeing John Jensen and Ian Wright in their suits and it makes you think. I think there was this feeling that the force was with us. [I didn't make the connection until much later as to whether this was a reference from Amy to the fact the game was played on 4 May which was all Star Wars fans know is 'May the force be with you' day. Even if it wasn't she was right, it did feel like there was something greater propelling us to victory. There wasn't of course but every Arsenal fan in the Parken that night – including myself – will tell you there was.]

Parma were a much better team. A much more sophisticated team, a much more able team than Arsenal were from a creative point of view, so that's another reason why 'One-Nil-to-the-Arsenal' was becoming ingrained. I'm sure the fans were singing it before the game in Copenhagen [Amy is right: my pals and I certainly did in the bars and streets of Copenhagen before kick-off. Testament not only to its anthemic qualities but also as a rallying call which embodied the never-say-die and resolute ethos of the team at the time.]

It's funny because I watched some of the footage again of that game and I was stunned at the quality of the Italians. Of how the gap between the two sides was far greater than I had thought at the time. [Again Amy is spot on. I watched the game for research purposes and just for old times' sake too and it was amazing how superior the Italians looked. Even twenty-one years on I was still worried we were going to concede an equaliser and lose the game late on] They were really a very good side. Which is why I really savoured Alan Smith's goal. It was pure celebration wasn't it Layth? It was a fantastic goal. It just goes to show that for all the gifts of Zola and Asprilla and Brolin, if one of them had scored it they would have been mighty pleased with it.

To have the immense back four and David Seaman, well Italian football was known for catenaccio but that night we showed them how to defend at the back too. They talk about the organisation of Italian Serie A defences but the Arsenal back line at that time was as good as anything around. [Although my shorthand notes of Amy's conversation with me don't show it, when I played my Dictaphone back I actually emitted a low growl in agreement when Amy said that. It was an instructive act which unconsciously showed the pride, I, and all Arsenal fans had in that back four at the time, and the satisfaction we took at shutting out better sides than us. And perhaps an even deeper subliminal response for those brought up on that side as an acknowledgement of the fact it's no longer the case]

I ask Amy an obvious question that had to be asked, 'How did you feel?' As a journalist myself I try to avoid asking people this in order to avoid a stock phrase or answer, but in the case of that final whistle blown in the Parken Stadion that night, signalling the culmination of heroic efforts by the team and management and the tremendous support Arsenal fans had shown the club, I felt it was a valid question to ask as I genuinely wanted to know. Amy replied instantly, 'Arsenal winning the European Cup Winners' Cup in Copenhagen felt magical'.

I asked, 'How would you put that achievement in context, the fact it is still Arsenal's second only European trophy'. At first I thought she misheard me in her one word reply, 'Exactly'. There was a silence for a few seconds as my brain made sense of what she was trying to say to me. 'Exactly', she replied again,

There's your context. You have to put it in the context of what people call the fourth place trophy. To qualify for the Champions League is a fantastic achievement by the club nowadays. By any club nowadays. So to do it for the number of years the club has, eighteen years in a row now I believe under Arsene Wenger is a really an amazing achievement. Certainly in the context of when you look around Europe to see how many other clubs have managed to do that run, I think it's only two other clubs so it's not easy.

The Champions League is very important to a club nowadays, but it's a totally different competition because it's a league factor. The Champions League is what it is which is you have a league situation for a number of months then it turns into a straight knock out in the later stages and the whole thing changes. But being in a knock-out competition from day one is a completely different angle entirely. So to win the 1994 European Cup Winners' Cup was really, really special.

Our interview is drawing to a close and I mention to the brilliant Amy that the book is to be called *The Miracle of Copenhagen*. I ask her to sum up the run and ask if it was indeed a sporting miracle that Arsenal triumphed in the Danish capital after one of the more unlikely runs in Europe. She thinks hard before replying, 'That's a tricky question. I think if we go back to what I first mentioned relating to Arsenal's triumph, what European football was then and what it is now, that is what gives the victory its resonance.' For me her answer sums Amy Lawrence up – thoughtful, articulate, insightful and passionate. But I ask her again this time more explicitly, 'Could Arsenal winning the European Cup Winners' Cup in 1994 be classed as The Miracle of Copenhagen?' This time she answers straight away, with the merest hint of irony in her voice, by saying, 'That's your line Layth'.

Publisher and founding editor of *The Gooner* fanzine, and a man who, along with Kevin Whitcher has helped me no end in my time as an Arsenal writer, and a lovely bloke to boot, Mike Francis recalls the night itself,

Hopefully you don't need me to detail the match itself, Layth, because my only memory of the action is pretty much limited to Alan Smith's winning goal. Reports tell me that it was a backs-to-the-wall performance throughout as we fought grimly to hold on to what we had. Ian Selley and Steve Morrow will not rank among the pantheon of talented midfielders to play for Arsenal, but they did the job they were asked to do on that evening and have the winner's medals to prove it.

The final whistle went and it was pandemonium in the stands. As you'd expect Wrighty was leading the celebrations on the pitch dressed in his club suit. John Jensen made an appearance waving his crutches around and George Graham strolled from player to player shaking their hands with a look which said 'never in doubt'. The trophy was presented on a hastily put-together platform on the pitch rather than high-up in the stand which was the norm in those days. Having been brought up on the tradition of climbing thirty-nine steps to the Royal Box at (the old) Wembley I recall thinking how odd it seemed. At least it was 'properly' presented to the captain and passed along the line of players rather than the disorganised and untidy 'huddle' we so often see today which I detest. Bah humbug!

I don't remember how long we stayed in the ground celebrating with the players and with each other, but I'm sure it was a long time and we had to be encouraged towards the exit by the stewards. Not before another rendition of 'One-Nil-to-the-Arsenal though'. I've got a feeling we walked back to the city centre and then it was on to a pub where much alcohol was consumed. Please understand that this was not because we wanted to, but because we needed to keep our throats well lubricated for the continuous singing which lasted well into the early hours.

Sharon and I did not travel back from Copenhagen until the Friday by which time the club had already held the open-top bus parade to Islington Town Hall, so we missed out on that. However, we can both say we were in the Parken Stadium when Arsenal won the Cup Winners Cup and it really was wonderful wonderful!

Jem Maidment's friend Chris Smith added with a smile,

When *Sky Sports* interviewed us before the game I remember giving, what I thought anyway, was the most concise interview that Sky interviewer had ever done. I mentioned how great Copenhagen looked on first impressions, my thoughts on the game, how I thought the match would develop tactically, comparing Zola, Brolin, Asprilla to Merson and Smudger. And you know what? Sky used none of it. But they did use my sleepy mate Eddie saying, 'It's a carnival atmosphere'. I know, twenty-one years on I should let it go, but ...

Jem himself recalls of that trip,

For some reason I remember being on the ferry to the Hook of Holland and it was packed solid with Arsenal fans. Loads of lads were drinking at the bar and passing this magazine around. I thought it was a porn mag or something, but it was *Loaded* magazine, which had just launched last week. [As an aside, having spent a month or two in the *Sabotage Times* office, run by the iconic former *Loaded* editor James Brown, I can only imagine the madness of working as a journalist on that publication which rode the zeitgeist of the mid 90s, and which I loved listening to James's memories of that time. One of my favourites being the time he went to Buenos Aries for a long weekend. But that's about all I can legally mention here ...] Everyone was banging on about this '*Loaded*', it was like nothing anyone had seen before. Football and girls all in the same magazine. After years of football being uncomfortable, unfashionable, violent and downright dangerous at times the sport was gaining a new image. The onset of the mid 1990s coupled with Britpop and Cool Britannia meant everyone wanted to be associated with the game that was dying, uncared for by all but a passionate crowd of dedicated supporters, supporters who are gradually being airbrushed out of the game now in favour of more shiny corporate hangers on without a clue of the passion that football gives you ... and more importantly what you must give football.

Jem was spot on in his recall on the energy of *Loaded*, and its triptych of football, style and attitude. Football was entering the twenty-first century in 1994. We just didn't realise it at the time. Even Nick Hornby wrote for *Loaded* back then. I remember him writing a colour piece on his experiences of Copenhagen including the memorable line (a play on Carlsberg's successful marketing campaign), 'Probably the best beer in the World' when he told the story of him and his friends passing the Carlsberg brewery in a pissed up coach full of Gooners. 'Was that the Carlsberg brewery? Someone asked. 'Probably,' came the deadpan reply.

Rose McGee's in Vesterbrogade became the official centre of Copenhagen for a few days, we even pinched a plastic Carlsberg beer barrel from behind the bar and brought him home. I don't think the owner minded too much, he must have made an absolute fortune and anyway, they love Arsenal over there.

It was a brilliant pub packed with Arsenal fans. The night before the game we were in there and there were the most amazing Danish girls. The most stunning of the lot, and Danes are very pretty people, came up to me and started talking. I was elated until she told me she really fancied my mate and would he go back to her house with her. Incredible. She really wanted him. In fact, she even offered to drive him back to Copenhagen the next day as she lived twenty minutes outside the city centre. But he wouldn't do it, because we had his ticket for the game and he was worried he wouldn't find us. I admire his loyalty to Arsenal, but you should have seen her …

One thing I do remember is finding a big box on a street corner after the game. It said 'Parma – 1994 Cup Winners' Cup winners'. Loads of Arsenal fans were buying up Arsenal t-shirts after the game, but the guy who printed up the Parma ones must have lost a lot of money. I wish I had kept one now. Chris Smith chips in with another memory, 'I do remember on the ferry across the channel my mate Alan Dyer tried to sell me his limited edition Swatch watch. He claimed there were only fifty made but at the very first BP station we refuelled in in Holland the fella on the till had the same watch!'

Jem then adds, 'We turned up having not slept for a day and a half, smelling awful. So we went straight for a beer and we all got interviewed by *Sky Sports*. It wasn't great telly but, incredibly, they aired it anyway. My mate's mum taped it and I still have the video somewhere, not that we can play it now.'

Jem's mate 'Sleepy' Eddie Odaro, who lives in London Colney recalls,

Five of us drove to Copenhagen in a battered old Rover – fans did anything they could to get there. The car was on its last knockings but, thankfully, it got us there even if we only had the one tape to play the whole way. We thought we'd get a hotel when we got there but we didn't have chance. So we were preparing to kip down in the car for three nights.

Then I met this Danish bloke who, incredibly, offered us accommodation at his parents' holiday home. For free. He was so trusting, maybe he took pity on us, but I just genuinely think he was a nice fella. He gave us the keys and directions and we all went back and had a shower and slept, for all he knew we could have turned the place over and stolen everything, not that we would have of course. Anyway, he returned later with his girlfriend and even cooked us a chicken stew. Then the phone rang and Jem picked it up. It was the parents. Suffice to say, they were not happy and we had to make a fast exit. Thanks Jem!

The perceptive Kevin Whitcher remembers the game as if it were yesterday.

Davis was definitely in the side. Brolin was the problem but he was slightly wide. When George Graham saw Paul Davis getting outdone by pace in midfield he immediately swapped the nippier Ian Selley with Davis to negate this weakness so our midfield three were Selley, Davis and Morrow, so that Selley could contain Brolin better.

Intrigued by the recollection I ask Stewart Houston what he can recall of the night and our tactics.

Parma were one of the top sides in Italy, Everyone remembers your Juve's and Milan's but Parma were one of the top sides in one of the top leagues, if not the top league in Europe at the time. And sometimes people forget that. Zola, Apsrilla, Brolin – top, top quality.

They were the favourites on the night. We were very much the underdogs. The mentality was if we can get a goal we would be very difficult to break down. If we could get the ball to Campbell or Merson out wide and Alan Smith in the middle we could create something. We felt on the night if we could get a goal we wouldn't then sit back and say come on we would look to push forward for a second. It wasn't our intention to sit back it was just the way it happened as they put us under a lot of pressure especially in the second-half. But of course we felt we would be very, very difficult to beat if we did go one nil up and the Italians were left chasing the game. We didn't have a lot of chances. Zola had a few chances but he didn't take them. Brolin had chances, they hit the post, hit the post and so did Asprilla.

I also have to say full marks to Alan Smith that was a smashing strike by the way. I actually had a look at that goal again in a bit of detail because I knew you were going to ask me about it. I obviously remember it very well at the time and watching it against reinforced what I remember on the night in Copenhagen. Alan Smith did very well. If you look at it in detail there is quite an indifferent mistake by one of their defenders. The Italian defender tried to clear the ball with a kind of scissor kick, a sort of over the head job, but the ball came more or less straight to Alan Smith. What Alan then did was controlled the ball efficiently and struck it with that left foot from the right channel on the edge of the box, it was just a classic goal. My thought at the time on the bench as soon as he struck it was, 'That's a goal'. It's gone in marginally just off the right hand post. You go back to luck a little, it could have just hit the post and gone out just as similar to Brolins hit the post and come out, but it didn't, and on the night its gone in. It's those small margins. But it was a terrific strike.

People look at the result and go lucky Arsenal again. But I don't think so at all. It was one of those nights where on the night you dig in and win the trophy. If you look back over those years it was part of Arsenals DNA, the capability to dig in and win important football matches and important trophies, look at when we went to Anfield. Everybody had more or less written us off that night, similar to Copenhagen, and we had to get two goals and we did it. We had that mentality where everything was possible. Everything and anything. We felt we could do it on any given occasion, that was our mentality and in our DNA.

Wining the trophy was such a huge thing. At the time of course but also looking back.

Kevin Whitcher recalls the day,

So in early May, Arsenal fans en masse travelled to Copenhagen, some by road (and ferry), some by air. There was no doubt that the majority of supporters in the city were English rather than Italian, even if Parma were the firm favourites to retain their trophy. And no wonder, with stellar names like Faustino Asprilla, Tomas Brolin and Gianfranco Zola, who had a record of converting a third of his free kicks into goals.

A then Gooner contributor, and soon to be editor of Highbury High, Tony Madden organized a trip for something like twenty people with flights and hotel. It was a two night stay, flying back the day after the final. On the first night there, Tony suffered from terrible toothache and had to retire early in agony, a real blow as everyone else was enjoying the beer in Denmark and having a roaring time.

The day of the game came around. One of our party, the Gooner's 'Highbury Spy' Steve Ashford, was desperate to hook up with Andy White, a mate of his from Bristol who was arriving by plane on the morning of the game. Long before many people had mobile phones, Steve just wandered around the centre for an hour or so hoping to bump into Andy, which indeed he did. We were all congregated in a bar that was a little off the beaten track so not completely rammed and settled there for the day, soothing pre-match nerves with a few pints. I recall the place was near a college or something and there was no shortage of attractive Scandinavian women cycling up and down.

Steve was not optimistic, feeling Arsenal would not be able to resist hot favourites Parma. Aside from being without Ian Wright, our stopper in chief John Jensen was injured, weakening the solidity of the midfield in a game that would require a great deal of denial of the opposition in this area. I took a different view. Although not confident, I certainly believed, based on the Gunners' will to win, that it was possible, even without Wrighty and Jensen. I had faith that a trophy could be won in a one-off match even if the opposition had better players. Will to win.

Time came to head to the Parken Stadium, with its weird office blocks in the corners separating the stands. The place was rocking, with I would estimate the Arsenal fans outnumbering the Parma supporters by at least three to one. Certainly, there were a lot of Gooners who had managed to get tickets in the neutral seats, in addition to the allocation the club had sold. It was incredible to think there were less than 34,000 people in attendance, given the amount of noise. Our seats were at a decent height behind the goal, in the upper tier of the Arsenal end, slightly to one side of the goal. Parma attacked us early on, towards our end and the vision of Tomas Brolin's attempt beating David Seaman and heading towards the goal will always stay with me. It was such a relief when it rebounded off the post.

Not too long after, Smudger's goal came out of nowhere, and sent all around me into ecstasy and more than one person at least two rows forward. I have no doubt a few knocks and bruises were suffered in that celebration, but it was worth it. The rest of the game was largely a question of old-style Arsenal backs to the wall although, in fairness, there were a few attacks and a couple of decent chances.

It was a long ninety minutes, featuring at least one very dangerous heart-stopping Zola free-kick at our end, and I would be lying if I said I enjoyed it too much. The chant of 'One-Nil-to-the-Arsenal' was sung long and loud many times and I am certain the support of the travelling fans helped motivate the team to keep going. It was an incredible atmosphere. The Parma fans, although well behaved before the game, weren't beyond pelting Nigel Winterburn with coins and probably worse as he lay prone in the penalty area at their end in the second-half receiving treatment from Gary Lewin. Such was the resolution of the side that George Graham only felt the need to make one change, bringing Eddie McGoldrick on for Merse in the eighty-sixth minute.

It was a case of tactics ruling the day. George Graham set the team up to stifle Parma brilliantly and when he saw early on that Paul Davis was getting done by the pace in midfield, switched things around so that the nippier Ian Selley played more centrally to be a more effective barrier. Both Selley and Steve Morrow are often derided by Arsenal fans these days, but both performed stoically in midfield in this game and without their contribution the win would never have been achieved. Both Merson and Kevin Campbell mucked in with Alan Smith playing a classic hold the ball up front man role. Due to injury he would only play a handful more matches for Arsenal but this was such a great night for him, reminding us of his qualities as a player. I am still astonished he is not one of the celebrated thirty-two players on the exterior of the new stadium, given his achievements with the club.

As for the defence, what can be said? The finest hour of the famous back five of Seaman, Dixon, Winterburn, Bould and Adams. Heroes all. I have no doubt that for neutrals it wasn't the finest match they would ever see, but let's face it, you could say that about a lot of European finals down the years. The full time whistle was a moment of triumph and ecstatic relief and we celebrated hard for at least half an hour before heading back into the centre to celebrate. Steve and I walked to the ground and back with Steve's long time mate Dave Wingate, who was suffering with cancer. No-one knew how long he had, but he would be buried before the end of the calendar year. 'They did it for me,' said Dave, as we chatted after the game. I can't swear that Dave ever attended another Arsenal match, but I am glad he survived long enough to see this one. He had one drink with us before returning to the hotel to rest up. If we felt drained, I have no idea how he managed to get through that day.

We enjoyed the celebrations in the same bar we had spent most of the day in before calling it a night. We heard the following morning the story of John Jensen on crutches joining a bar full of Arsenal fans and getting up on a table to lead the chanting. Both he and Ian Wright had celebrated with the players and the fans after the final whistle, the latter dressed in a suit, while the Dane was in a tracksuit looking every inch the stereotyped Scouser with his trademark moustache. Jensen apparently lost his wallet during the celebrations at the bar, which was unfortunate to hear.

The morning after, we dragged our exhausted but ecstatic bones to the airport, and who should we see in the departure area waiting for a flight, but Tomas Brolin. Out of sheer respect we didn't rub it in, but for the width of a post, there was a man who could have denied one of Arsenal's greatest nights, and one of the best experiences following the club that I, and I am certain, many other Gooners, have enjoyed.

My friend Matt Bleasby who we eventually met after the game recalls the trip,

Guy and I arrived in Copenhagen a day before the final having decided to save a bit of money by camping. It was clear from the hour and half train trip out from the city centre this was not going to be an option after the final, we decided we would try and crash on Layth and Mozzy's hotel room. So we decided on a quiet night of consuming the duty free rather than heading off anywhere. Ironically the campsite was the only place where we saw any Italians. We went past a campervan and a seemingly lovely old Italian couple invited us in.

Sharing their Italian red, genuine Parma ham, and perfectly cooked pasta, in return I think we shared some duty free cigars. We tried conversing in broken French as a common language as their English was as poor as our Italian. However, unfortunately, as the evening progressed it became clear that the lovely old couple held strong views that could only be described as right of Mussolini. As much as we tried to steer the conversation back to the upcoming final, it went all Italian UKIP (or BNP at the time) and they started on about lazy southerners and immigrants which we should have taken exception to but were far too polite. 'We meet here after the final' they said to us as we made our excuses to leave. I remember Guy and me muttering under our breath as we left them, 'I don't bloody think so you bunch of old racist fascist's – but thanks again for the dinner!'

On the day of the final we were all supposed to meet Mozzy and Layth and Mozzy's brother Mark at the main station in Copenhagen. Now the station has two entrances and we managed to both pick the wrong entrance (my version) or I picked the wrong entrance and didn't wait (the author's version). However as we waited we chatted to the growing numbers of Arsenal fans. It was clear that a large contingent, probably one in every three were Scandinavians out of what felt like around 60,000 Gooners assembled on the day.

The Swedes and Norwegians we met were in good form and spirits and spoke perfect English. So, of course, as all English abroad do after a few beers, Guy started initially talking slowly and loudly so they could understand. A few of them offered us chewing tobacco, it didn't mix well with the beers and was promptly spat out! On other days they might have taken offence but everyone saw the funny side. The conversation eventually even moved to a normal pace and volume as Guy gave up trying to make his broken English understood to people who spoke our mother tongue perfectly. The local Danes were equally friendly and keen to join in the fun and get behind John Jensen's team. It seemed like Arsenal had the freedom of the city as the bars and side streets filled up with Gooners everywhere getting steadily drunker.

The police didn't seem to be bothered as along as it stayed good natured (which it did from what I saw) the only time I noticed the police having to do anything was when the Burger King accidently burnt down just off the main square. The Arsenal love in carried on at the stadium with the DJ seemingly playing 'Go West' on a loop, in an effort to further encourage the Arsenal contingent to sing the 'One-Nil-to-the-Arsenal' and 'We'll-win-because-we're-Arsenal'. It didn't really need that much encouragement considering it had been sung all afternoon around Copenhagen. It was clear that everyone wanted an Arsenal win. I even remember the late Jeremy Beadle coming out on the pitch and waving to the fans just to add to the whole parochial nature of the final. I wouldn't want to argue the comedic merits of Beadle's output, but I'd be surprised if anyone outside of England had heard of him, and if he was allowed the freedom of the park at a European cup final then anything seemed possible, so why couldn't Arsenal beat a star studded Parma side

The facts are well-known, Parma had nine internationals going to the upcoming World Cup in America (in which the Italians reached the final) whereas Arsenal has just one, and that was Eddie Mdcgoldrick. But at the time during the match I can honestly say I don't think any of us thought the result would be in doubt, although it may have been self confidence in part helped by the invisible cloak of alcohol. Looking back now after The Miracle of Copenhagen it seems in retrospect dangerously blasé to assume that the night would end in triumph, but it just felt right at the time, thanks to a bit of luck and Alan Smiths strike.

The post-match piss up was brilliant. It was very good natured – in contrast to the UEFA Cup Final of 2000 in the same city, and every bar was rammed full of very happy, very drunk Gooners. The locals again were joining in too, in part to celebrate John 'Faxe Beer' Jensen's triumph, even though he didn't play, and part just to enjoy watching the English enjoy a raucous celebratory drink. We eventually met up with Layth and Mozzy in a bar in the post-match celebrations.

I seem to recall Guy had a night to remember by doing his bit to cement Anglo/Danish relations with a rather attractive local girl to cap off a perfect night. But as he always said: 'If you're going to celebrate, then celebrate in style'.

Builder Mark Langley recalls the post-match celebrations somewhat differently,

I'd been to every game home and away on that run. I flew to Odense but can't remember too much about it, the final on the other hand was a different matter. In the days before the internet and booking hotels online we flew out to Copenhagen but just couldn't get a hotel room for love nor money. I'd been out to see us win 1–0 in Turin in 1980 when the late Paul Vaessen hit a late winner, which incidentally saw the Juve fans go mental at the tiny band of Gooners in the crumbling Stadio Comunale, they were throwing anything they could get their hands on, but we simply didn't care.

Of course we lost the final in Heysel against Valencia so it made it doubly sweeter for me fourteen years on in 1994 to see us lift the Cup Winners Cup in Copenhagen. I'll always remember the scenes afterwards, but unfortunately what I'll also remember is being pig-sick at the airport the next day. As we didn't have anywhere to go in the middle of the night we went back to the airport as we were flying back the next day. However, I picked up a stomach bug, I still maintain to this day it wasn't the alcohol it was a grotty hot dog at the stadium at half-time that did for me. So it was a bit ironic that on one of the most special nights in Arsenal's history I spent it cramped up on a really uncomfortable bucket seat without a back of course trying to avoid sh*tting myself! I actually camped near to the a set of airport bogs in the middle of the night so I didn't have a long trek to use them, but it seemed like half the Arsenal fans in the airport along with me had the squits too! I can still remember the smell! Looking back it was funny but at the time I was more concerned with holding my bowels together than the afterglow of Arsenal actually winning the Cup Winners Cup!

Loyal Gooner, north Londoner and cabbie Nigel Maitland recalled the trip in his own memorable style, explaining to me,

We went from Luton Airport a couple of days before the match. This time I went with Dave (Lillywhite), Paul Williams and Lincoln. After a few beers in Luton Airport and a few more on the plane we got to Copenhagen quite early. It was here that I probably made my first mistake of the trip and produced a litre bottle of vodka which we drank while waiting for the bus taking us to the hotel, The Cab Inn. Yes, I am a cab driver and I was staying in a cabin. Anyway we checked in and went out on the lash. I had been a bit wary about going away with these three because, although they liked a beer, they were very interested in smoking the funny fags too but to their credit they stayed out all day and night and we got suitably hammered. Mark joined us later on. He had come under his own steam because he had a girlfriend he could stay with in Copenhagen. Great, another funny fag fumer.

Our excuse was that Arsenal were playing in a major European Final, probably against superior Italian opposition in Parma and without Ian Wright and we were nervous. We spent quite a lot of time in a hovel called The Spunk Bar which I had come across thirteen years earlier en route to an England World Cup qualifier in Norway (yes, that one).

Its only attraction was that it was markedly cheaper than everywhere else and sold funny drinks in test tube style containers. We never did find out what exactly was in them but they got the job done. The next day the lads just wanted to 'chill out' in the hotel (which to them meant smoke funny fags) which to me was torture so I consoled myself with a few takeaway beers and another bottle of vodka. I can't really remember much of the rest of the day as it all got a bit blurry. Lincoln reckoned I had passively smoked half of his dope.

We eventually started heading for the ground and stopped in a bar fairly close to it and started chatting to some Arsenal fans. One group told us that their mate had a pilot's license and had flown them over by private jet and was flying them back straight after the match. We asked them which one of them was the pilot and they pointed to a middle aged bloke unconscious in the corner. We wished them luck and headed for the ground. The game was a bit of a blur but I remember Arsenal fans far outnumbering Parma's and being fantastically noisy throughout a nerve jangling 1–0 win. I don't think I've seen Arsenal fans going as potty as we did when Smudger scored. After the game I think everyone was physically and mentally drained and we ended up in some strange venue watching/listening to an even stranger band. The next thing I knew we were waking up in The Cabin and it was time to go home.

Dave Seager added,

For the final I watched it at my mate's flat and I had a quirky superstition back then. This was when I had to watch the TV I would do so with the volume on zero and to listen to the Capital Gold commentary. The main man on Capital Gold back them was Jonathan Pearce, now of course on *MOTD*. I just loved his ludicrous bias towards London teams on his London Radio station and decided he was lucky for the Arsenal the previous season when he commentated on our remarkable comeback against Leeds. The amazing comeback was inspired by Paul Merson and Pearce's 'The Magic Man Merson does it again!' is still a favourite line in sports commentary for me. Anyway Pearce did it for me again as Alan Smudger Smith score the winner against a far superior Parma team littered with superstars. Not forgetting we were without our own superstar Ian Wright. Another case of course of scoring one and holding out and no one did that better than our famous back four.

Loyal Danish Arsenal fan Flemming Christensen also explained,

For the final we went with approximately fourty people together, and had a great day again.

It was with a lovely atmosphere and no bad feelings between the clubs at the places where we went. Some of us had families with them and we had a great couple of hours before the game with songs and happy faces. I am just sorry I don't have any pictures, it would have been nice to remember such a special day.

Tim Payton added just how much The Miracle of Copenhagen meant to him,

Arsenal's 1994 Cup Winners Cup Final win holds special memories for me as my first ever time of watching Arsenal away in Europe and what a final it was. Arsenal were definitely underdogs, something we'd known from the moment Ian Wright was shown a yellow card during a tense semi-final win over PSG which ruled him out of the Final versus Parma. This was the era of the famous Arsenal defensive back-line and the semi-final win was an archetypal one for what was to become a familiar anthem at Highbury – 'One-Nil-to-the-Arsenal'.

Copenhagen is still a vivid memory and easily finds it place right at the top of an all-time Arsenal list of matches for me. I recall the sense of occasion, and the noise from the Arsenal fans who easily outnumbered travelling Italians. And the nerves as Arsenal somehow clung on to an early Alan Smith goal to record a famous victory.

Once again the 'One-Nil-to-the-Arsenal' song rang out defiantly to match the efforts of the team. It was our way of saluting and encouraging our amazing defence and indeed the defensive efforts of all eleven on the pitch as everyone had their role to play. But it was more than just another song. It was our proud rebuke to those who didn't like the way that Graham had moulded a defensively disciplined team that relied largely on the brilliance of Ian Wright and occasionally stalwarts like Alan Smith.

'One-Nil to the Arsenal' in Copenhagen was the summation of the George Graham era and really did define mid-1990s Arsenal as Arsenal secured a rare European triumph.

Arsenal author Jon Spurling also gave a thoughtful insight into that night into Copenhagen in terms of the current era. He told me, '1994 and all that! Much though I've admired the skill and finesse of Wenger's teams over the last eighteen years, I like one thing even more is a winning Arsenal team. And if it's 1-0 like it was in Copenhagen, then that's fine by me.'

Darren Epstein added,

We should never have won that game. We didn't have Wright, and they had Brolin and Asprilla. Two massive world stars but they were so intimidated by us that they couldn't play their game. They kept giving the ball away, for some reason we just intercepted everything and when Smith scored, they were in a panic. We'd blown a few finals, so some of us just kind of froze counting the minutes down. Smith had been on somewhat of a barren run, Wrighty had taken up his mantle as number one striker and Alan became more of a support striker to lay the ball off – but he was a great team player.

In fact he's one of my all-time favourites, so the fact he scored that goal was just fantastic. We won of course, and I think it's fair to say that for all the beer that is made in Denmark that Copenhagen that night was drunk dry by the Arsenal fans.

Steve Tongue who was covering the final as a BBC sports producer explained to me,

> Both legs of the semi-final against Paris Saint Germain were probably a very good rehearsal for the final because Parma, even if they were less well known as a club, had the more gifted individual players.
>
> I remember speaking to another journalist before the game and agreeing that Parma might well be too good for them. The fear was that if they scored first, they could then pick off Arsenal on the break. But of course it was Alan Smith who got the goal and there was another superb defensive performance from then on.
>
> Overall in the campaign one of the most impressive things was how some of the unsung midfield players like Hillier and Morrow and Selley came in and did a job. And apart from those strange Liège games you could say it was a classic George Graham campaign.
>
> A great shame that it all ended so badly for George thereafter.

The respected Tongue was right. It did end badly for Gorgeous George which was a real shame. But for Gooners everywhere we will always have our memories of the days when it ended well. When it ended magnificently. Such as The Miracle of Copenhagen.

Parma had never even appeared in Serie A until four years before in 1990. The shrewd coaching of Nevio Scala and the financial backing of Italian diary heavyweight Parmalat (now there was another story that ended badly) saw progress accelerate in the early part of the decade. Parma qualified for Europe for the first time in their history in 1991, won the Italian Cup in 1992 before triumphing in the Cup Winners' Cup in 1993 when they won at Wembley against the Belgians of Antwerp. Then through the money of a magnate called Calisto Tanzi (who made his fortune with UHT which allowed dairy products a longer life) bought Brolin, Asprilla and Zola to the club. Therefore with Arsenal weakened by injuries to key men, as well as missing the important Martin Keown as a man-marker supreme and the hugely influential Ian Wright through that heart-breaking suspension incurred with the booking he picked up at an anguished Highbury against PSG, the Gunners looked mere fodder for the Italian aristocrats. Or so everyone outside of our wonderful club thought.

For those experts on reading between the lines of what George Graham would say about his opponents before the game his pronouncements were a master-class in highlighting the areas he thought could be attacked, but at the same time appearing to praise his opponents. Was it any wonder even Alex Ferguson himself would try and not get too involved with our canny Scot who was more than a match for the Govan bruiser in the early to mid-1990s. Graham artfully explained, 'Parma are a great team of individuals. They can play only one way, the coach gets his players to fit the same system, whatever side he picks.'

The sub-text was clear. George was effectively saying, 'Your fancy stars won't like playing against us, for we are a united team the likes of which you haven't encountered in Europe'. Graham continued, 'The greater the odds against us, the better we seem to perform'. It was a masterclass in psychology. It was also a rallying cry (to his team and to the fans who were starting to believe a miracle could take place) by evoking recent past glories and the collective spirit they roused by being the underdogs in such famous victories.

George added,

It happened in my first final as manager. When we beat Liverpool to win the 1987 League Cup, and it happened again two years later when we won at Anfield to win the league. This is the sort of quality foreign teams respect. Continental sides are wary of British teams. Parma know they're going to be in for a tough game. And no, my team haven't practiced penalties because I don't want them to entertain negative thoughts. We are going to do our best to win this game, and in the process win Arsenal's second European trophy.

George, as ever in big matches called it perfectly.

Early on in the game Asprilla looked to work some of his magic but Bould clattered into him and won the ball. It was important not just because of the strength of the challenge. It was deemed legal after all. No, it was the fact it was perfectly timed. If the Italians thought all they had to do was turn up this momentary but juddering cameo persuaded them otherwise.

The somewhat nonchalant attitude they took to the previous night's training at the Parken when they appeared so dismissive of Arsenal as a team of footballers was now replaced by the dawning realisation they were in for a terrible battle.

The doubts that cameo raised reinforced George's assertion that they were a team of great individuals, with the unsaid narrative being they weren't a great team when the going got tough. And it would be tough against this fired-up, proud, Arsenal side who were fighting for their teammates, their friends, their badge and their loyal supporters who had trailed across Europe with their last pennies, giving their all in following them around the continent. There was too much at stake to give in now, everyone had sacrificed so much and if the atmosphere was at fever pitch then that's because everyone knew that after this there was nothing left to give. The players had given everything, and my god so too had us supporters in our own way.

'We are The Arsenal', as a youth coach said, passing those immortal words on to the late, great David Rocastle. A man who could still leave a lump in the throat of those who knew him, and a catch in the voice of those who idolised him, 'Remember who you are, what you are, and who you represent'. Even now as I write that line that means so much to so many Arsenal fans my eyes water slightly and my throat catches as the powerful resonance it instils. As the crowd roared their heroes on make no mistake, for that last match on that immortal run, a word that produced so many cherished memories, my word it made you proud to be a Gooner.

Such is the capriciousness of sport, and football, margins between success and failure are invariably gossamer thin. In the thirteenth minute (unlucky for some) Zola, who had played with the god Maradona in Naples as a youngster, in a blink of an eye played the ball through Arsenal's central defenders and formidable twin pillars, and onto the path of Brolin. He was through. He had to score, and if he did score it could not be 'One-Nil-to-the-Arsenal' on the night for so many reasons. As Brolin went to shoot never have I heard such a collective intake of breath, for we all knew our strengths lay in defending. If Parma were to go one-nil up early on it would leave us vulnerable on the counter in seeking parity, and for such tactically and technically able players it would allow them to pick us off at will. The match depended on this moment.

Brolin shot in front of the massed ranks of travelling Gooners stationed behind the goal including Mozzy, Nige and me and a myriad of others. The ball flew past Seaman headed for the net. But somehow the football gods had been pleased with Arsenal's offerings to them that season. They decided in their wisdom to make the ball bang against the post and trickle away to safety. For me that was a much a defining moment of the game as Alan Smith's goal. Even now when Arsenal fans discuss that game they will mention the fact Brolin hit the post. As if that explained everything.

Seven minutes after that, Dixon took a throw around 40 yards out from the Parma goal. Minotti, who had been touted as the next Franco Baresi, did what Baresi would never do and ill-judged a defensive clearance by trying to be too clever by half. Baresi was stylish but he was also pragmatic, and an ultimate team player. He would have fitted in well at Arsenal. He certainly wouldn't have done what a self-indulgent Minotti did and attempt an overhead clearance wide left of his box. Not only that but launch high and back towards the danger area and towards an opponent.

Alan Smith, who looked at me as if I was mad when I asked him what was going through his mind at that particular moment in his existence, chested the ball down, and with his left foot, hit what was the best shot of his life, the most perfect volley of his career. Ultimately it was one of the best goals in a red and white shirt. Bucci the goalkeeper made an attempt to save it but the ball hit the inside of his post and went in – as opposed to trickling out after striking the inside of the post.

It was a great goal that launched a roar from our travelling support as loud as any in our long and illustrious history. I recall tumbling down over seats as people cascaded along rows united in a celebration that was as joyous as it was unexpected. Once the initial pandemonium subsided somewhat there was only one thing to do, bellow out 'One-Nil-to-the-Arsenal' as loudly as ever. It was a bellow of triumph, it was a rallying call, a clarion cry to rouse underdogs and steel them for the long night ahead. It was an iconic moment that will never be forgotten by those who were there or by those who cherish the history of their beloved club.

Arsenal stood firm for the rest of the game. It became a battle of endurance for our team, although as Stewart Houston told me revealingly, 'It wasn't our plan to sit back, it was just the Italians attacked us. That team of "great individuals" threw wave after wave of assaults on us but we held firm.'

David Seaman, Lee Dixon, Tony Adams, Steve Bould and Nigel Winerburn kept their shape, held their nerve and worked as hard as they did in their lives to keep the scoreline 'One-Nil-to-the-Arsenal'. Ian Selley, Steve Morrow, Paul Davis, Kevin Campbell, Paul Merson and of course, Alan Smith were all heroes on the night. In a performance that spoke of a team that never knew when they were beaten, and resonated with the fact that they might sometimes have been outnumbered but would, never, be outgunned. When Mr Krondi of the Czech Republic finally blew his whistle at the end of the second-half (a second-half fraught with tension and the fear we would concede) the stadium erupted as an outpouring of relief turned to the realisation that Arsenal had won the European Cup Winners' Cup against all the odds.

We had won the trophy. The Miracle of Copenhagen was complete.

Jill Armstrong is the daughter of Arsenal legend Geordie Armstrong. A lovely person very much in the essence of her father: dignified, understated, loyal, an extremely helpful person with a caring nature – and Arsenal through and through. Her father Geordie Armstrong played 621 matches for The Arsenal, scoring sixty-eight goals for his beloved club. He was a person loved by everyone who came into contact with the modest County Durham born man. He was, is and always will be a true Arsenal legend. Not least because he was only one of two men who had links with the pair of European trophy wins by The Gunners in their history twenty-four years apart.

On 31 October 2000, the much-loved Geordie Armstrong collapsed after an unexpected brain haemorrhage while at a club training session. As a sign of respect a pitch at Arsenal's training ground in London Colney is named after him in his honour in a fitting tribute. Jill, who took some time out of her busy schedule told me,

I know for sure Dad would have been delighted for the boys to win the European Cup Winners' Cup trophy in 1994. He was always quoted as saying how great it was to see the lads win trophies, as he knew how that felt as a player when he won trophies with Arsenal, including the club's first European trophy, the Fairs Cup in 1969/70.

In 1994, he knew the boys deserved to win in Copenhagen after the incredible run they had in that season's competition, bearing in mind the very good sides they beat along the way, and I know for a fact he would have felt very proud to have been involved as a coach during that season.

I know he would have enjoyed *The Miracle of Copenhagen*.

Gooner fanzine stalwart Steve Ashford, better known by his moniker the Highbury Spy recalled the trip movingly,

Copenhagen 1994. Arguably the greatest night in Arsenal's history alongside Anfield 1989. Again we were the underdogs and no-one gave us a cat in hell's chance of bringing the trophy back to London. I wish I could say 'the famous old trophy' as the Champions League is often referred to but the Cup winners' Cup would do for us. We hadn't won a European trophy since 1970 and that was nearly a quarter of a century ago.

The odds were against us with opponents Palma from Italy having some of the world's best players at the time such as Zola, Asprilla and the tricky Swede Thomas Brolin. Arsenal were without talisman and hero Ian Wright who was suspended and several first choice midfielders.

We had the 1990s equivalent of Abou Diaby, Ian Selly and Steve Morrow in midfield. The latter is in Arsenal folklore as the scorer of the winning goal in the 1993 League Cup Final against Sheffield Wednesday and he's apparently a lovely bloke and an Arsenal fan to this day, but in my humble opinion one of the worst players ever to wear the Arsenal shirt. But that night Selley and Morrow did their jobs, hassling and pressing the Palma midfield to give our magnificent defence some respite from the almost perpetual bombardment we were under for most of the game.

I was at the match with a load of mates too numerous to name here but we had a fantastic time in the cities myriad bars the day before the match. As with all finals all the blokes you haven't seen for years turn up and act like they've never been away!

One of our crowd was a quiet, studious guy called Dave Wingate. A lovely fella who I met in The Lord Napier, a jazz pub in Thornton Heath near Croydon, where Dave lived. One night in early 1978 I'd gone with Ian and Colin McCarthur who were teachers and they knew a fellow teacher who was with Dave that night. Dave and I were both Arsenal fans and we hit it off immediately although I have absolutely no idea why as he was university educated and quiet and I am a bit ebullient to say the least, and the height of my education was at Barnhill secondary Modern in Hayes, Middlesex which is now a housing estate – although you'd probably get a better education in a two bed terrace than at Barnhill anyway!

My equally uneducated mates thought Dave was too posh for us to hang around with but he opened my mind to politics, current affairs, social history and all sorts of other topics we enjoyed talking about. Dave was a marathon runner, didn't smoke, didn't drink or eat much and lived a very healthy lifestyle. Unlike me who smoked, drank to excess and got a curry down at every opportunity. In the car coming back from away games during the interminable drives down the M1 Dave used to lecture me about my lifestyle saying I would drop dead by the time I was fourty if I didn't stop drinking and going out every night. I thought he was right but I didn't change my ways. Dave carried on running and not drinking and driving.

I remember one day in the Compton Arms in 1993 Dave said to me when we were in the loo taking a p*ss that he was going to the doctors the following Wednesday as he'd had a pain in his back for a week or two and it was getting worse. He went for tests and the next time I saw him the poor guy told me that despite his clean living and healthy lifestyle, the consultants had told him he was suffering from cancer which had spread to his lungs and other organs and he had six months to live.

Dave and I had enjoyed a great relationship from 1978 and he had managed to beat the doctor's odds and stay well enough to attend the Cup Winners Cup Final in 1994 and we were sitting next to each other on the plane and then the coach on the way to the city centre the day before the match.

My first thoughts on leaving the airport were that there were no houses in Copenhagen. Just block after block of dull un-inspiring council flats and all of them had a bright green pot plant or two in the front window. Must be a strange Danish custom. That night we had the most wonderful time ever. Just about every Arsenal fan I knew had made the trip to Copenhagen and we partied long into the night. Somewhere at home I have loads of pictures of us all in team groups holding flags and banners and smiling and having the time of our lives. I stand out because I had my first ever number one crop the day before we flew out and these are the first (but sadly not the last) pictures of me with the sun beaming off my 'chrome dome'! If I can dig them out maybe they'll make the second edition of this book!

Anyway, at one stage I remember our crowd of mates and acquaintances numbered around fifty and half of us were upstairs in one bar in a tiny alley and the other half were upstairs in the bar opposite and we all hung out of the windows with our flags and scarves and beers and almost touched each other across the sky. Oh how we laughed and sang Arsenal songs until well into the night. We had to enjoy ourselves as Parma were going to thrash us the next day and this was our chance to have some fun.

At the Parken, the atmosphere was unbelievable. Arsenal had two thirds of the ground. Parma had the upper tier of the other end and that was it. Maybe the fact it was like a home game for us helped us overcome the overwhelming difference in class between the two sides, although we did have the famous back four on show that night, Dixon, Bould, Adams and Winterburn plus David Seaman in goal, so we had a chance. And so it proved. After Brolin hit the post early on and Seaman had made some magnificent saves, it happened. Alan Smith unleashed a thunderbolt and it went in off the far post and crashed almightily into the net. Cue pandemonium! To this day I have never known a goal celebration like it. I was on the end of a row in the lower tier of the main Arsenal end and I ended up hugging a complete stranger and rolling all the way down the aisle steps right to the front of the terrace. We were in ecstasy. Even now, talking about this I've got goose bumps.

You know the rest Layth. Arsenal held on, the back four and Seaman were superb. Even Morrow and Selly were magnificent. Against all the odds we had won our second European trophy and the party could begin again. I remember Tony Adams would hardly let go of the cup and Arsenal's PA hosting for the evening, played 'One-Nil-to-the-Arsenal' time and time again as the players paraded gloriously in front of us with the gleaming silver trophy. I will never forget that night.

Back in Copenhagen I hooked up with Dave again as we had been separated on the way back from the stadium to the city centre. Goodness knows how anyone met up in those days as mobile phones were not generally available for another two or three years, but we did. I remember running towards Dave and he had the biggest smile on his face I had ever seen. Draped in his 1971 silk scarf that he always wore to finals we hugged and he yelled at me 'They did it for me Steve, they did it for me!' He knew it would be his last final and the last trophy he would ever see. Five months later in September 1994, Dave passed away.

He was 43. I miss him to this day. How Dave would have enjoyed the Bergkamp, Robert Pires and Thierry Henry years. The countless trophies we've won since. The last years at Highbury. The Emirates. Life can be so cruel but that night in Copenhagen It did Dave a small favour. They did indeed 'do it for him'.

In the country where Hans Christian Andersen was born, writer of fairytales, 'One-Nil-to-the-Arsenal' was never more apt than in the Miracle of Copenhagen.

Ben Ansell was a good friend of mine. And of so many. Intelligent, loyal and fun-loving, he was a fantastic son, brother, partner, pal. And a huge Gooner. He turned twenty-two during that run and loved watching Arsenal clinch their unlikely place in history. Unable to get to many of the games that year he cheered his red and white heroes from afar before later moving from Monmouthshire to London for work, and to support his beloved Gunners. He meant so many good, fine and decent things to so many people, and his memory and spirit (not to mention his love of Arsenal0 will live on in the memory of all the people whose lives he touched in so many ways.

When he tragically died in a car accident at the age of thirty-three (the same age as a hero of his, David Rocastle, which is truly no age at all) in July 2005, he left a gap in so many of the lives he sadly left behind. At his funeral, in which more than 500 people turned out to pay their respects to him and his dignified family, his coffin was draped in an Arsenal flag.

I am proud to call him my friend and I always will be. I still think of Ben a lot, as everyone who knew him, did, and still does. Especially when I recall all the matches we went to together with a large group of friends (who when we get together still raise a glass in his honour even now) including Arsenal's Champions League away games in Europe. We also had joyously riotous times following England away all over the world including the international tournaments of Euro 2000, Japan 2002 and Portugal in 2004. I remember one time over a late-night drink on a trip to

Katowice in 2004 to watch England take on Poland in the grim Silesia mining belt in a World Cup 2006 qualifier the year before he died, we somehow got onto a conversation about Arsenal's 1994 European Cup Winners' Cup run. 'I still can't believe we won it', he told me filled with the happy incredulousness he, and I, and countless others shared about that triumph. But instead of moving on to talk about other football topics, I vividly recall he was genuinely more interested in hearing my experiences, asking me, 'What was it like mate? It must have been brilliant following Arsenal around Europe the season we won the Cup Winners' Cup.' I was too drunk, and too inarticulate (while also believing we would have a lifetime to talk about such a season) to explain properly to him, so I simply said, 'It was a bloody miracle'. Ben then simply lifted his glass of vodka and red bull which he always supped when the hour was late and drink had been taken, clinked mine in a sign of what I took to be mutual friendship and respect, and replied with a smile, 'It must have been'.

Ben Ansell. True friend to all, and true Gooner. I hope this book answers your questions about The Miracle of Copenhagen.

Rest in peace, mate.

Acknowledgements

I owe many people so much in the course of writing this book. Firstly I would like to thank my friends and colleagues at *Archant on the Comet* newspaper and the Royston Crow for their support and good humour in getting me over the finish line. A big nod of appreciation goes out to one of the finest court reporters in the UK, big Olly Pritchard (for those who know what MacNae means look out for him in the next edition after he managed to overturn a section 11). Also to the placid but deadly accurate James Scott, Becca Day, formerly of the parish of Glasgow, now Royston's best-ever reporter (not only for her brilliant Italian translation of the *Gazetta della Sport Torino* match report, but also for her truly awful attempts at a cockney accent which kept my spirits up when toothache and tiredness made me flag). My news editor, the forensic Nick Gill, who has forgotten more about proofing than most will ever know, and whose feedback I really appreciate. The lads on the sports desk, Mark Hemmings, Damian Roberts (it's still not too late for Barney to become a Gooner mate) Mike Edwards and Tom Sharpe. And of course *Comet and Crow* editor, and one of the best newsmen in the entire UK, not to mention surely the hardest working person in journalism and the most passionate too, Mr John Francis, to whom I owe my career in the this trade I love.

I would also like to thank Sky Sports Johnny Phillips, for his loyal, unwavering support when I needed it, Guillem Balague for allowing me an insight into what it takes to be a top-level football journalist and for coming along to my book signing in Hitchin Waterstones and buying my previous book, *Arsene Wenger: 50 Defining Fixtures*, Gracias. (Don't forget to keep an eye on his football revolution at Biggleswade United). I also have a huge debt of thanks to pay to Duncan Hamilton, previously of *The Sun*, now a brewer, which is as fitting a trade as a former Fleet Street journalist can opt for. As well as the, dare I say it, tech-obsessed editor of the vibrant *Rugby World* magazine, Owain Jones, even if, as a passionate Welsh egg-chaser his capacity for drinking is woefully poor.

I'd also like to thank Owen Blackhurst for supporting me when I first started out, for believing in me and showing me that anything was possible, and for encouraging me to blag a pre-Champions League press conference with Zinedene Zidane. Thanks also to the genius that is James Brown, as the former editor, I hope you enjoyed the *Loaded* references as much as I enjoyed my time at *Sabotage Times*, playing darts in your office, drinking far too much and learning an awful lot about social media. It's no wonder people of the calibre of Sam Diss, Rachel

Krishna and Carl Anka graduated from your madcap office to *Buzzfeed*. Thanks also to the guys at *Talksport Warm-Up* for all their help with promoting my last book and my sports writing in general, as well as the exceptional Gary Parkinson at *Four-Four-Two* magazine.

I also have to say a huge thank you to Will Gore, deputy editor of the *London Evening Standard* and the *Independent* for all his ongoing support and advice. Likewise, the *Standard's* brilliant online sports desk editor Amar Singh, and his trusty lieutenant Tom Dutton for all their help in allowing me freelance shifts when we both can find the time at Derry Street, and for publishing my work.

My appreciation must also go to the fantastic Shevon Houston, formerly of the NCTJ, and her father the hugely impressive Stewart Houston; and Joanne Butcher of the NUJ, NCTJ and JDF. Joanne and Shevon I can only apologise for plugging my last book at the end of my speech to the Director General of the BBC and other assorted luminaries at last year's JDF. I blame it on the wine.

A big thank you to the gang down at Tip TV, Commander in Chief Nick 'The Moose' Batsford, Serge Braga, and Nigel Seeley, for allowing me on their ever-growing show to spout my usual nonsense on football and cricket. Also a big thanks to *The Roar Sports* down under, the incomparable Geoff Lemon, Cam Fink and Tristan Rayner for allowing me to further my cricket writing (as well as filming an interview with me after a miserable Arsenal home defeat for Foxtel).

A massive thank you too goes out to the wonderful Amy Lawrence for all her perfectly articulated insights and help with the book. For someone so busy, not to mention so well-established, it says a lot about her that she was willing to waste her time talking to me. As ever my heartfelt gratitude must go to the legendary Patrick Barclay, who again has helped me progress my career no end by simply allowing me to listen to him and his lifetime of incredible footballing experiences. Thank you so much Paddy for being a mentor … I still owe you that pre-match pie down at Piebury Corner too.

Mention must go to fellow Amberley author, vastly experienced journalist and producer, and a really good guy to boot, Steve Tongue. Not only for his support and encouragement, but also for unearthing a couple of gems I used in the book. Thanks Steve, I owe you big time.

Thanks to the legend that is Alan Smith for his time and spell-binding insights into Arsenal Football Club, the 1993/94 run, George Graham and so much more that form the basis for this book. I'd also like to thank Ray Parlour for his time when I interviewed him for the *Evening Standard* last year, as well as Perry Groves for sharing his views on George Graham via an interview I conducted for *The Gooner*. Thanks also to Josh Landy for facilitating our conversation last year, and of course to the kind-hearted Jill Armstrong who was such a help, and for her kind tweet about my young daughter Josie on FA Cup Final Day who wore a yellow ribbon. Thank you Jill. I know so many people are proud of your dad as an

Arsenal legend and a great man, but I also know, as a father myself, that equally, he would be very proud of you.

Recognition must go to Dan McCarthy for setting up the interview with Alan Smith, I'm looking forward immensely to our collaboration on our forthcoming book *What The Arsenal Means To Me*. And of course to Paul and Nicky Campbell and all the gang down at Piebury Corner for all their support with my last book.

I would also like to thank everyone who shared their memories of Arsenal's stunning 1993/94 European Cup Winners' Cup run and triumph. Credit must go to (in no particular order): *The Gooner's* finest Kevin Whitcher, Mike Francis, Steve Ashford; Tim Stillman of *Arseblog*, Tim Payton of AST, Arsenal shareholder Darren Epstein, *Gunners* authors Jon Spurling and Dave Seager. And Ampthill's finest Jem Maidment, formerly of *Sky News*, and his pals Chris and 'Sleepy' Eddie. See you all for pre-match beers on me next season, and thanks for putting up with my constant hectoring in getting you to file copy. Thanks also to the utterly brilliant creative genius that is Paine Proffitt for the superb Arsenal image he painted just for this book. I'm looking forward to the original artwork hanging proudly in my study/writing parlour/shed soon. Thanks must also go to everyone at my publishers Amberley, and in particular my exceedingly patient publishers Amberley Publishing.

A big shout has to go to some of my oldest and most loyal friends, Guy 'L'Homme Sage' Wiseman, Matty 'Beaker' Bleasby, Stephen 'Mozzy' Moszoro, 'Ginger Mark' Langley and Nigel 'Nige' Maitland who kindly shared their memories of those wonderfully happy and carefree days. Although not in the book, I have to say a massive thank you to Danny 'Cheese' Jimenez and his fantastic wife Gina and lovely kids Hannah and Rachel for their constant support which has kept me going at times when I faltered, and not least for Danny and his girls coming to my book signings and acting as cheerleaders. I'd also like to thank another old schoolmate Chris 'Bosley' Keane for putting me onto the effortlessly cool PSG fan Antoine during a Test Match at Lords. I'm not sure anyone in the Compton Stand during the recent New Zealand game could quite work out what a Frenchman was doing watching a cricket match while talking about Arsenal's 1993/94 ECWC run. While we're on the subject of the French, a big thank you to my father-in-law, and Jack Nicholson lookalike Patrice Aurrouseau and his lovely wife Mimi who always gave me encouragement to pursue a career in writing for a living even in the dark days.

I'd also like to thank Tess and Sophie Ansell for allowing me to dedicate this book to their beloved son and brother Ben Ansell. I only hope you think the end result is good enough to justify your faith in me. All my love as ever.

An acknowledgment must go to my brother-in-law Jamie Street who is doing a fantastic job in raising my three nephews and nieces, Ben, Ellie and little Olive, after the tragic loss of our much-loved and desperately missed Anne Aurousseau, who fought so hard, and so bravely, for so long, against her dreadful cancer. Thanks also to Pauline Mason, and Andrew and Sandra Street.

A huge thanks must also be paid to the wonderful wider Hitchin community who rallied around our family when we needed them the most. You know who you are, and to those special people who have my complete and utter respect and gratitude, my family and I will forever be in your debt for your kindness.

To my parents as ever for all their help, love and understanding, and for my dad being tough as old boots in surviving everything life throws at him, and for them always being there for me unconditionally. (And for my Donegal-born mum asking me which position Arsenal finished in the FA Cup).

Finally, to my long-suffering partner Claire Aurousseau and our three beautiful children – and Junior Gunners – Charlotte, William and Josie. We are blessed to have such happy and healthy kids who are blossoming before our very eyes. And of course for the fact they are huge Gooners who ask the most sensible questions, including a pearl from our youngest Josie, who I took to the 2015 FA Cup Final and who asked me afterwards, 'Dad how bad are Tottenham if we beat Aston Villa 4–0 and they beat Spurs?' (How bad indeed Josie.) To Claire, who has held the fort remarkably, and been the one person who has supported me and believed I could be a journalist and author from day one, when so many others doubted me while showing unbelievable strength amid such sorrow in losing her best friend and sister Anne. I owe you everything. I hope you can forgive my absences during the writing of this book, you truly are a special person and for that I will always be grateful. You have my complete love and utter respect.

Layth Yousif, Hitchin
Friday 5 June 2015.